W9-CQP-469

CAN YOU TELL A VRM FROM A WRAP-AROUND MORTGAGE?

If you can't, it will probably cost you money—and quite possibly the house you want.

In the real estate market of the 1980s, the hard truth is that what you don't know will definitely hurt you when you're buying a house. Now, at last, this invaluable guide makes the most complicated jargon completely clear, and shows you how to use every "trick of the trade" to give yourself the vital edge in bargaining for the best price and then financing your purchase on the most favorable terms.

Now you can talk to bankers, brokers, and house-sellers on better-than-equal terms. Now you can find sources of ready money and big savings that you probably don't even suspect exist. Now you can learn all that you need to do to get the house you want.

HOW TO BUY
YOUR OWN HOUSE
WHEN YOU DON'T HAVE
ENOUGH MONEY!

RICHARD F. GABRIEL, one of America's top real estate brokers, is the author of *The Complete Guide to Building A Real Estate Fortune In Older Multiple Dwellings*. He is president of his own private real estate holding company, Angel Realty, vice-president of Gabriel Brothers' Sales Organization, and owner of numerous residential and rental properties in Florida and New England.

Recommended MENTOR and SIGNET Books

HOW TO BUY YOUR OWN HOUSE WHEN YOU DON'T HAVE ENOUGH MONEY!

by Richard F. Gabriel

A SIGNET BOOK

NEW AMERICAN LIBRARY

TIMES MIRROR

TO MY LOVELY FAMILY—
Faith, Suzanne, Steven

PUBLISHER'S NOTE
This publication is designed to provide accurate and authoritative
information in regard to the subject matter covered. It is sold with
the understanding that the publisher is not engaged in rendering
legal, accounting or other professional service. If legal advice or
other expert assistance is required, the service of a competent professional person should be sought. The concepts introduced in this
publication should be reviewed, before being acted on, with a local
competent professional person because of the wide variation in
different local customs and/or regulations.

Published by arrangement with Prentice-Hall, Inc.

 SIGNET TRADEMARK REG. U.S. PAT. OFF. AND FOREIGN COUNTRIES
REGISTERED TRADEMARK—MARCA REGISTRADA
HECHO EN CHICAGO, U.S.A.

SIGNET, SIGNET CLASSICS, MENTOR, PLUME, MERIDIAN AND NAL BOOKS
are published by The New American Library, Inc.,
1633 Broadway, New York, New York 10019

First Signet Printing, February, 1983

1 2 3 4 5 6 7 8 9

PRINTED IN THE UNITED STATES OF AMERICA

PREFACE

This book can give you the knowledge and techniques you must have in order to buy your house with as little of your hard-earned out-of-pocket cash as possible. The dollar-stretching techniques you'll learn in this book could very well make the difference enabling you to buy *today*—not in some distant tomorrow—your own home so that you can enjoy it and profit from its appreciating value.

Too many young couples, single people, and retired couples are finding themselves forced out of the home-buying market because of the increasing prices of homes and the ever-increasing amounts of cash needed to complete these purchases. Inflation, which in one form or another will be with us for years to come, will continue to increase the price of homes and, consequently, more and more people will be hard-pressed to come up with the money to buy their own homes.

This book will give you the techniques—the guidelines— that will help you handle this situation that appears so discouraging to potential home buyers. These dollar-stretching ideas could very well make the difference for you, as they have for thousands of others, in terms of buying your home *now*.

Let's face it: if you picked up a trombone, it would be unrealistic for you to expect to play a tune on it without learning what to do. Remember when you sat behind the wheel of a car for the very first time? You were unable to drive off into city traffic because you had not as yet learned what to do. It takes knowledge and expertise for you to become *either* a trombone player or a car driver. In much the same way, you have to know the techniques and gain the knowledge it takes to get the most mileage out of your limited dollars in order to buy a home. You have to be familiar with the guidelines that you can use in buying a house advantageously, particularly when cash in the bank is an important factor. It is this specific help that this book offers you.

If you're like most Americans, a house will probably be the most expensive purchase (whether the price is $40,000, $75,000, $200,000, or higher) you'll ever make. In light of the importance of this purchasing decision and the dollars involved, smart potential buyers will want to learn all the possible cost-cutting techniques available.

In a nutshell, this book will offer you dozens and dozens of techniques that will help you conserve your hard-earned out-of-pocket cash so that you can buy your own home and not go broke in the process!

CONTENTS

CHAPTER ONE

HOW TO
RAISE THE MONEY

That house you thought was beyond your pocketbook can become a reality if you know the proper buying techniques.

In this book we will be showing you (1) dozens of ways to raise cash for either all or part of your down payment, (2) dozens of creative financing techniques that will show you how to make your home purchase a reality, and (3) a host of other techniques that will help you to stretch your home-buying dollars in these cash-shy days of the 80's.

All these techniques and tactics are legal, moral, and, of equal importance, proven and tested in today's marketplace. Because these techniques are being successfully put to use now, thousands of buyers throughout the country are finding the procedures to buy a home now that otherwise might have been beyond their financial grasp.

Alert real estate brokers, too, are increasing their familiarity with many of these financial techniques so that they in turn can be of greater help to their buyers and/or sellers and, in the process, complete more transactions. It goes without saying that the more you make yourself familiar with these approaches, the better you will be able to work with your real estate broker or salesman, for an informed buyer is a better buyer.

If you're looking to buy a house in today's market, your most important consideration will be your ability to raise cash and/or structure the total financing of your purchase. To put it another way: You could spend every weekend for half a year or more letting real estate brokers show you all kinds of properties suitable to your needs as to size, neighborhood, and other features but unless you have a very good handle on how you plan to swing the financing of your purchase, all you'd be doing by looking at properties is sightseeing and putting yourself on the road to possible disappointment and frustration. Chances are, if you're like the vast majority of potential home buyers today, the two troublesome areas, financially speaking, that stand between you and your ability to buy a house will be raising all the cash for the down payment and/or working out a mortgage loan arrangement that you can live with.

These two areas, now probably more than ever in light of the continually escalating prices of houses, are the biggest stumbling blocks for most prospective home buyers. When the availability of both sufficient cash and affordable mortgages become roadblocks in this way, then you, as a potential home buyer, should keep two things in mind:

First, you will be well advised to assign much more of your time to the financing and home-purchasing process. Gone are the days when you could run down to your local friendly savings bank or savings and loan association and, with a moderate amount of cash and a liveable mortgage from the bank, you would soon be

2

moving your furniture into your dream house. Those days of easy cash, easy mortgages, and low-priced houses have disappeared before our eyes right along with cheap electricity, low-priced gasoline, and affordable oil bills!

It is just because of this change in the cost of things that you will have to put in the extra time and effort in order to work out how you're going to handle all the financing of your purchase. You would be well advised to set aside a minimum of four to six months, if not more, just to work out all the financial foundation of your home purchase.

The second thing to keep in mind is that you will have to do your homework and learn every tactic and technique you can get hold of if you truly want to buy a home in today's real estate market. You've heard it before and it applies especially to today's home-buying market: Anything worthwhile takes time and effort. For most people, the purchase of a house is probably the biggest, and most important, financial undertaking of their life, so by and large most people are—or should be—willing to learn what they can do in order to make their home an affordable reality. It will behoove you to read and understand thoroughly the dollar-stretching techniques we'll be talking about before you run off and look at houses. There will be time enough for you to get excited by eye-appealing, three-bedroom, two-bath houses with cute kitchens, charming fireplaces, and lovely landscaped grounds! First and foremost, give yourself ample time to learn and apply the dollar-stretching, creative financing techniques in this book.

CREDIT: THE HOME BUYER'S GREATEST ASSET

The first financial hurdle for most home buyers struggling to stretch their limited dollars is the problem of coming up with all the cash needed as part of the down payment.

The two major sources for you, as a working person, to increase your cash reserve are your present income and a second income.

YOUR PRESENT INCOME

Notwithstanding how inflation has added to all our daily living costs, tests have been conducted showing that savings of 10 to 20 percent can be effected by all of us. Frill items, overpriced foods, unneeded impulse purchases are areas that most of us squander needed dollars on. However, if we programmed ourselves to "pay" ourselves first by putting into a savings account a certain amount of money every week or month (no matter what the amount), and stuck to a regular schedule so that it became a habit (like paying our monthly rent, phone, and electricity), then the dollars would mount rapidly. Unfortunately, most of us work in reverse: first we pay our rent, food, utility, transportation, leisure pursuits, movies, and so on, and then, if anything's left—and there usually isn't—we put it away on a strictly catch-as-catch-can basis.

Will this regular savings program be difficult to do? You bet it will, but perhaps three things might make it easier for you, as they have for the thousands of other working people who have put their minds to homebuying.

1. Cut out a picture of a house (like the style you'd want to buy) and post it where you can see it readily.

Every time you make a savings deposit toward your house purchase, mark it down on a chart next to the picture of the house. As the check marks, and the dollars, increase, you will gain in determination and momentum in your dollar-saving project.

2. Keep your savings book readily available. Every time you add something to it, look at the dollar additions posted. As you see these regular additions begin to build, your enthusiasm for your goal-oriented savings program will follow. Although the amounts are quite a bit smaller, I know many people, myself included, who take pennies, nickels, dimes, and quarters out of their pocket every night and put them into paper rolls that banks supply. At the end of the year, through regular deposits, these coins have grown to hundreds of dollars! Say what you will, old Ben Franklin knew what was right for us.

3. Your track record of success in a regular savings program will help to bring you two important things: ready cash and a favorable impression when you go to a lending institution to borrow funds. There isn't a banker in the world who will fail to be impressed with your financial self-discipline, an important factor when a banker makes the decision when you seek a personal loan.

CASH RESERVES BUILT BY SECOND INCOME SOURCES

Today thousands of home-hungry buyers-to-be are adding to their cash reserve by holding down second-income, moonlighting jobs. Weekend jobs and after-work evening projects are bringing in extra dollars. Many people are beginning to realize that their hobbies and other interests or talents can be translated into extra dollars. If you have a talent or interest in any of a variety of things such as foreign languages, math, playing the piano, art, crafts, photography, skiing—you name it—you're a natural to pick up dollars in after-hours tutoring or teaching. Perhaps you're good with people: many local businesses can use part-time sales or office people. Look through your Yellow Pages and it will give you a host of job ideas, or go to your public library and ask to borrow books on moonlighting and second-income jobs. These extra dollars, if you sock them away in a savings account as soon as you get them, can quickly add up. Equally important, your self-evident determination to work toward a given goal (that is, to increase your savings toward a home purchase) will be looked on with great favor by almost any lending officer when you want to borrow. After all, when you add dollars to your savings through your own hard efforts, you're giving a valuable clue as to your character. Lending banks loan money on the basis of how they view you in light of the four C's. The first "C" stands for your available *Cash*. The second C stands for your *Character*, the kind of person you are in the eyes of a lender. The third C stands for *Capacity*, your ability to repay a loan as prescribed. The last C is for *Collateral*, an asset you might have to secure, or stand behind, a loan. These four C's come together to help form a lender's opinion of what kind of credit they may want to extend.

Credit, or the right to defer payment for goods or services, will be an important part of your financial life. It is vital to your being able to borrow funds to buy your dream house. And establishing your credit with a bank, whether you're fresh out of college, new to the financial world, or a wife who's failed to establish a financial

6

identity of her own, is much more simple than most people envision.

The two quickest and simplest ways to establish a financial credit history are as follows:

First apply for and get a charge account at a local store; a retailer or a department store. Make small purchases, pay for them promptly, and, by so doing, you'll be helping to develop a favorable financial track record for yourself. Also, apply for and get a charge card in your own name from one of the bank cards such as Master Charge, or VISA, or one of the travel and entertainment cards such as Diners Club, Carte Blanche, or American Express. Establishing credit in your own name is imperative, a fact that some wives have yet to fully act on; less than 20 percent of the major charge card members are women. Charge cards, used with discretion, offer you ready identification, a receipt for your purchases, and an excellent opportunity, through prompt payment, of helping to establish a record of responsible repayment of debt.

Second, open up a checking and/or savings account at your bank. To vastly speed up your credit image and your standing as someone who repays loans promptly, you can use an acceptable and legal technique that has helped many people establish favorable credit:

Open a regular savings account at a bank—it could be as small as $300. After a short while (a week or so) go to the same bank, ask for a $300 loan (ask for six to twelve months to repay it), which you will then secure by this savings account (that is, the bank will hold your $300 savings account passbook as collateral for the loan). Because the bank's $300 loan to you is secured by your savings account funds, they will not even need a credit check on you.

Now go to another bank, and with your $300 loan do

the same process over again (that is, open a $300 savings account and make a $300 loan secured by the $300 savings account). You now have established lines of credit at two banks which is the basic purpose of this process. Then go to yet another bank and open a personal checking account.

You started your credit-building process when you opened your first account. Now you will take the most important step in this credit-building process because you will begin to pay off each of the loans with your own checks, using the $300 you have deposited in your new checking account. As you pay off your loans (and you'll probably be making an early repayment on your loan, thus making your banker happy), you "unfreeze" the $300 passbook funds, which you'll then use to pay off both loans early.

Let's review what you've been able to accomplish toward building bank credit:

1. You now have had two savings accounts, each for $300.

2. You now have two bank loans, each for $300.

3. You now have an active checking account.

4. You now have established credit at two banks by virtue of having paid back your two loans.

In the eyes of the experience of the two lending banks, you have proved yourself an excellent credit risk, a fact that will give you a good rating for future bank loans and for credit bureaus who might seek financial information on your credit standing.

A few thoughts about this credit-building technique. It can be done with any amount of money, whether it's

8

$300, $500, $1,000, or whatever, and the entire process should take approximately three to five months (that is, normal procedure is to wait a minimum of three days for a check, such as your $300 savings account check, to be posted in the banks). Although the banks will be charging you their current rates on your passbook loans, bear in mind that you'll be getting one of the lowest loan interest rates because your loan will be collateralized (secured) by the most liquid collateral there is, namely, the cash in your passbook, and your passbook account will be earning interest even though the bank will actually be holding your passbook until your loan is paid. Furthermore, you will be prepaying your loan (rather than letting it run for the full time of the loan), thereby further minimizing the interest cost to you. Finally, the cost to you of this loan interest is a legitimate deductible item on your income tax.

However, the most important thing for you to remember is that for whatever small net loan interest costs you will incur, you will have put yourself on the road to establishing important credit with two banks in your community, and you will have accomplished it for next to nothing in cost (the difference between the interest earned from your savings account and the interest charged on the passbook loan is minimal, particularly in light of what it's accomplished.) With credit now established from your favorable loan pay-back record, borrowing money for just about any purpose, even getting a personal loan on your signature alone, becomes a favorable reality.

BORROWING: THE CASH-SHY HOME BUYER'S GREATEST TOOL

With credit established, you've laid the foundation for your ability to borrow money and, frankly, when you don't have enough money to buy your dream house, one of the most important avenues open to you will be your ability to borrow the additional needed cash. Or, as a real estate investor friend of mine who successfully buys houses and small rental properties put it: "I don't need cash to buy . . . only *access* to it."

If, like many people, you may have hang-ups about borrowing money, perhaps some of the following concepts might shed some new light.

First, borrowing funds that will aid in the purchase of a valuable asset, such as a well-selected house that appreciates in value, is completely different from borrowing funds for consumer goods (TV sets, furniture, foods, etc.) that generally deteriorate, lose their value, or get consumed.

Second, prudent borrowing of funds for a worthwhile appreciating asset is a morally sound, financially sensible procedure used throughout this country by both members of the business community and millions of private citizens as an acceptable means to acquire something of increasing value. The only time borrowing is "inadvisable" or questionable is when the individual borrows excessive funds knowing he will not be able to repay his debt, or when the purchased item will have a short useful life and the debt (that is, the obligation to repay the borrowed funds) will linger on for months or years beyond the useful life of the consumed item.

Third, the cost (the interest) of your borrowed funds

is a legitimate tax-deductible item that can be used to reduce your personal taxable income.

Fourth, when you borrow money during inflationary times, such as our country is currently experiencing and will undoubtedly continue to face for the foreseeable future, you will be paying back the money to the lender with *cheaper* dollars. These will be cheaper dollars because they will buy fewer goods in the future when you're paying them back. Being a borrower and paying back in cheaper dollars during inflationary times is, in many ways, smarter than being a lender, who gets paid back a fixed amount with dollars that have no upward adjustment to account for their lost purchasing power. The soundness of borrowing in inflationary times is particularly true if you're buying an asset such as a well-selected house that appreciates and, in turn, moves up in its market value at a pace somewhere near the rate of inflation. This is just what happened in the 70's and it could well be the same in the 80's in many areas throughout our country. According to a *New York Times* article, an informal sampling of 200 executives puts the anticipated average annual rate of inflation at about 10 percent for the 1980's, which is about the same anticipated average rate of market appreciation in homes for that period.

In a nutshell: Debt, in an amount you can financially handle, is not a four letter word! On the contrary, prudent borrowing to buy an appreciating asset, such as a house that you will repay with cheaper dollars, makes good sense. Businessmen and real estate investors have used borrowed funds (that is, other people's money— O.P.M.) to begin, build, or expand their business or investment activity. Now, more than ever, you should look at the purchase of your home in the same light as a businessman or investor would.

HOW AND WHERE TO BORROW

LIFE INSURANCE

One of the best sources of cash available to you will be a loan on the cash value of your life insurance policy. Depending upon when they were purchased, these whole life policies make loans available at interest rates between 5 and 8 percent, which, considering current rates, represents an outstanding value. Thousands of interested home buyers have used this source of relatively inexpensive money in order to raise the funds they need to buy their home. Contact the insurance broker who sold you your policy and he will arrange all the required steps for you and answer all your questions. If you choose to make payments on the interest you'll be incurring on these borrowed funds, remember that they are a tax-deductible expense. However, if you elect *not* to pay these interest payments when due, the insurance company simply adds the unpaid interest to the loan amount by deducting it from the policy's remaining cash value. You will then be paying interest on this interest.

Borrowing at bargain rates on the cash value of one's life insurance has been one of the best sources for substantial dollars for thousands of cash-shy home buyers in our country. A 1981 article in *Changing Times*, the Kiplinger publication, indicated that current policyholders have approximately $120 billion in untapped cash value to borrow against at favorable rates. Make this one of your first possible sources of financing to help you buy your dream house.

PERSONAL LOANS

One of your best sources for needed cash to complete a purchase of a home is a personal loan from a local lending source such as a savings bank, a commercial bank, or a savings and loan association. Commercial finance companies such as Beneficial, ADVCO, and Household Finance also are possible sources but their rates are usually higher than those of banks.

Personal loans (rather than business loans, which are more involved and harder to get) are one of your quickest means to get needed cash. A bank's decision as to whether to extend you a personal loan is based primarily on those four C's of banking (Cash, Character, Capacity, and Collateral). Let's look at these four categories more closely as they might relate to you.

CASH. The lending bank will look at the amount of your available cash. Hopefully, through your increased savings and moonlighting efforts you will have been able to add to whatever cash reserves you have. If you can show the banker that you've been adding on a regular basis to your savings account, you will gain some Brownie points. Don't be discouraged if you're not sitting on a big fat chunk of cash—if you were, you certainly wouldn't have felt the need to buy this book and, more important, you probably wouldn't be considering borrowing dollars at an interest cost to yourself. Your cash position is only a part, and not necessarily the most important part, of the overall picture that a bank loan officer will look at when deciding to extend you a loan.

CHARACTER AND CAPACITY. The kind of person you are and a bank's feeling about you are important. If you've been able to save money regularly, tell the bank *in detail how* you've been able to do it (that is, through a monthly habit of savings and/or overtime work or a second job). Your banker can't help but be impressed with these details as they will give him valuable insight as to the kind of person you are and therefore the kind of borrower you could be. If the bank perceives you as reliable and trustworthy, your chances of getting a favorable loan decision will be greatly enhanced. The bank will make its evaluation based on:

1. Your track record in making prompt payments on department store charge accounts, credit cards, and other charge account areas or lenders.

2. Character reference that you may have been able to get from employers or town officials who have known you or with whom you have had any kind of financial dealings. If you've borrowed money from a friend and have paid it back as arranged, he or she might be approached to write a letter of recommendation for you.

3. The way you handle yourself at a loan application interview. Be prompt for any bank appointment. (A 30-minute-late arrival at your first loan officer date might make him or her wonder if you'll also be late making loan repayments.) Also, be neatly dressed. First impressions are still important, and if you look neat and businesslike, then your appearance will encourage the banker to want to do business with you. Answer all questions in a direct and pleasant way. Finally, be prepared to answer certain basic questions you'll be asked:

(a) How much do you want to borrow?

(b) How long will you need it for? With a personal loan which might be extended to you on your signature alone, you could request 12, 24, or 36 months, but this will vary according to bank policy, economic conditions, and how the bank views you as a risk.

(c) How do you plan to pay the loan back to the bank? Your *capacity* to repay a loan is of prime importance to a bank. You should have this answer pretty well thought out in your mind in as much detail as possible before your loan application visit (for example, "I plan to take X dollars out of my monthly income," or "I'm taking on a second income source that will provide X dollars"). If you have a second source of funds to handle the loan repayment, so much the better; that will further increase your standing in the eyes of the bank. However, this is not a necessity—unless you come across to the bank as "Jesse James" or have had serious problems meeting previous repayment responsibilities to other creditors or lenders.

HINT: It will not only help the loan officer tremendously, but it will also help create a favorable impression about you in his eyes if you come in with *both* names and actual account numbers for any savings deposit accounts, checking accounts, and credit card accounts you might have. You will then look that much more like a well-organized, on-the-ball kind of potential customer that the banker would be interested in doing business with. Character and Capacity are important bank considerations, so give it your best, particularly if you're light in the cash department.

COLLATERAL. A bank will prefer to make a personal loan where they see that you have collateral (that is, some kind of security to back up the loan), but this is not always a necessity. Liquid collateral (something that can be transferred into cash readily in a matter of days, such as stocks, bonds, savings books) usually gets you a preferred interest rate on a loan in contrast to nonliquid collateral (real estate, vehicles, furniture, collectibles, etc.).

HINT: If the banker asks you for collateral, offer an asset you have that would be approximately the same dollar value as your loan request. Don't offer all your collateral assets, as he just might take them all. Bankers like *all* the security they can get, but you may need one of these other collateral assets for another loan at a future date and then you'd be up the creek if you'd already pledged all your available assets.

Personal loans are usually made for things like household furniture, consolidation of bills, vacations, travel, educational costs, auto and home repair, medical or emergency expenses. If you request the loan for helping to finance the purchase of a home, you might or might not meet a favorable reaction, depending on the philosophy and degree of conservatism of the bank. For example, suppose you needed $10,000 cash down to buy a house and you had $6,000 and therefore were looking for a $4,000 loan. Many banks might review only your ability to repay the $4,000; conversely other banks would review your ability to carry all the current financing and all the carrying costs of a house in today's market plus the additional carrying costs of this $4,000 loan. By today's market we mean that a lender used to look only at the potential borrower's ability to handle P.I.T.I. (Principal and Interest on a mortgage, plus Taxes and Insurance). Now, however, with skyrocketing home heating costs, some lenders feel the need to ascertain if the borrower's finances can also handle these extra energy costs before granting the loan. Some people will take out a personal loan on a dual basis: that is, part to be applied to one of the above purposes and the balance toward buying the home. However, this kind of consideration has to be an individual decision.

By and large, lenders are more interested in your ability to repay your loan in light of all your other monthly financing responsibilities than they are in the actual purpose of the loan. What it gets down to is how the bank *perceives* you: your track record with other financial repayment responsibilities, your capacity to meet new loan repayments, and possible collateral you might have to secure your loan (although the consideration of collateral might be less important than your track record and your financial ability to meet your new loan responsibilities).

Your loan, particularly if it's a signature loan—meaning it's backed up by no assets but only your word that you'll make repayment as arranged—may require a co-signer, who could be a member of your family or a friend. If a co-signer is requested, offer the services of only one co-signer, even though you might have more than one available. Why? You might need the additional co-signer for another loan some time in the future, so don't exhaust them both on one loan application.

HOW TO FILL OUT YOUR PERSONAL FINANCIAL STATEMENT

Ask your bank to give you a copy of their personal financial statement form. They will be happy to show you how to fill it out. Here are some tips in connection with filling out this form in order to put your best foot forward:

1. Each bank has its own personal financial statement form. Do not use the form from Bank A to make a loan application to Bank B. Although the financial information would generally be similar, each bank feels more comfortable with its own form (some banks are like jealous loves: they want to be the only one in your life). Banks, by the way, normally do not check with each other for credit references on a loan application; they do so only if you've given their name as a credit reference.

2. Having a telephone is an important consideration to a lending bank when reviewing your loan application. It shows that you have some roots and that you're not a wandering vagabond but can be reached if the bank needs to contact you. Also, the presence of a telephone indicates you're at least paying your telephone company bills fairly promptly; otherwise, they'd shut off your phone service.

3. You should be able to show residence for a minimum of six months. However, if you've just moved to your present address but you lived in your previous residence for a number of years, bring this out in your loan interview. Bankers look for continuity and steadiness in the place of residence, personal income, and debt repayment. Put another way, one thing loan officers are *not* comfortable with is uncertainty.

4. If you have had serious financial problems in the past, the lender will uncover them. Be frank and open with your lender and bring out these problem areas *before* he discovers them, thereby avoiding the impression that you're trying to cover them up. If you bring out these things first, the lender might think better of you. He might say to himself, "This guy's trying to level with me. Possibly I can trust him and that's important in my loan considerations."

5. When you list on the financial statement the assets you have, don't forget to include the following:

(a) Coin, stamp, gun, or antique collections or other collectibles of value.

(b) Any contracts, lease arrangements, or fee arrangements that indicate dollars owed to you for goods or services rendered. As an illustration, in my role as a business consultant, I mentioned this fact to a young couple filling out their financial statement in preparation for a loan request. I stimulated their thinking: they had completely overlooked the fact that the wife's brother-in-law was staying at their home and paying rent of $40 a week.

(c) Any investment you might have in a product or service, even though it has not yet reached the marketplace. It has an asset value that should be reflected in your personal financial statement. Examples are a contract on a book to be published or a patent on a product to be marketed.

(d) If you are a craftsman, the replacement value for any sizeable collection you have of hand or power tools.

(e) Campers, vans, boats, recreational vehicles, motorcycles, and the like.

(f) Antiques, family heirlooms, jewelry, and similar possessions.

(g) Payroll plans, stock options, and/or co-contributed pension plans, money invested in bond or stock funds, Christmas Club funds, and so on.

6. Don't overinflate the value of assets. Bankers have their antenna up on large amounts listed for home fur-nishings and the like, particularly if the listed value seems out of whack with the borrower's general life style. Furthermore, if you're already a home (or vacation retreat) owner, overinflated prices will probably catch the banker's eye. For example, if you showed a house value of $85,000 with only $25,000 insurance on it, the loan officer might think that either the house's market value, as listed in your financial statement, is over-priced or your home is vastly underinsured. If it's under-insured and if you had a fire, you would have to invade your other assets in order to raise funds to rebuild; this in the eyes of the bank might seriously jeopardize the chances of the bank loan being repaid as arranged.

If you follow these suggestions relating to the prepa-ration of your personal financial statements, you'll stand a better chance of securing a loan.

BANKS AND BANKERS

You can speed up your search for successful bank-borrowed funds by being familiar with the different types of conventional lending sources. Your choices are:

• *Commercial banks:* These are primarily interested in, but not confined to, short-term loans to individuals or corporations (one to five years or less). Sometimes they can be recognized by the word "trust" in their name, such as The Weston Bank & Trust Co.

• *Savings banks* also known as mutual savings banks: These are basically in the field of mortgages for single-family, owner-occupied homes and home improvement loans.

• *Savings and loan associations* also known as thrift institutions: These are basically in the field of residential (home) mortgages, small rental properties and limited commercial properties, and improvement loans.

The distinctions between the banks (short-term personal loans) and the savings banks and thrift institutions (long-term real estate loans) are becoming blurred inasmuch as each of these lenders is now moving into the other lenders' category and offering loan services to new kinds of customers. Therefore, your best bet to speed up your time in looking for a loan is to ask local businessmen, accountants, attorneys, and real estate brokers which local banks (*always* get as *many* banks or thrift institutions' names as you can) are usually interested in granting loans.

Because personal loans are a great source of profits, more banks are after this business. This is an important benefit to you because if you fail with your loan request to your first bank, immediately do two things:

First, ask the first bank's loan officer *why* the loan was not granted to you.

HINT: Ask for details. In light of today's consumerism, the banker is pretty well compelled to tell you why the loan was not favorably considered. The denied loan applicant can insist on a written Denial Report spelling out exactly why he was turned down.

Second, go to the next bank that makes personal loans and make out a loan application and, if possible, incorporate anything you might have learned from your earlier loan application at the first bank. They may have been tight for lending money when you applied or they may have had mixed feelings about how steady your career-income area was, or perhaps they were concerned about your family's two-income source inasmuch as your wife is in her seventh month of pregnancy, or they may have had misgivings about some blemish or questionable credit report they got back concerning you. If you're not able to get the first bank to reconsider their initial turndown in light of any additional insight and assurances you give them, then waste no time getting over to bank number 2, or 3, or 4. The point is this: different banks look at different loan requests quite differently for different reasons. Each bank has its own changing money needs, costs, and philosophy, and consequently, each bank could very well judge differently the desirability of extending you your loan.

Do not be discouraged if a bank does turn you down. (It's about at this point of frustration when you begin to believe in the old saying: Banks are the places that give you loans if you're successful in convincing them that you don't need the money.) Banks, by the way, do not make their loans on the basis of *your needs*, they make them on the basis of *safety* (that is, whether they will get their money back) and *yield* (the amount of interest they can expect to receive on your loan in comparison to other loan areas they could put their money into).

Keep in mind that the big bank buildings with their impressive entryways, monumental columns, marble floors, potted plants, fancy desks, and the like are merely trying to impress you through their outward appearance that they are solid, stable, reliable, and a good trustworthy place for you to place your money with. They are designed to intimidate you ever so slightly, but enough so that you'll feel a little cowed by their might and power, which puts them psychologically in control and you on the defensive.

22

HINT: Where possible, try to deal with a local, independent community bank that advertises that they "serve the people" rather than with a large conglomerate bank. And don't be hesitant to point out to the local bank that advertises they're there "to help the community" that that is precisely why you've selected *their* bank to do business with!

So do not let yourself be thrown by all this architectural razzmatazz. Look at it this way: banks have a commodity called money that they want to interest you in. However, if you don't like bank number 1's offerings, then you can do your business with the bank down the street. Remember, you and millions like you are the very lifeblood of banks, for they *need* and *depend* on you in order to get a source of money, through deposits, and in order to have customers to make safe and profitable loans to in order to use those deposited funds.

Perhaps you might find it helpful to think of this when you go into a bank to make a formal loan application: When you're sitting at the loan officer's desk, although your palms may be sweaty, your stomach may be bouncing, and you're probably wishing you were a hundred miles away, think of the pleasure and joy you'll receive from the use of your borrowed dollars, and the fact that the loan officer might be as nervous as you because he's been put on the carpet by his boss twenty minutes before for not bringing in enough new loan business. The only difference between you and him is that he can hide behind his fancy desk while you're sitting in front of him feeling as exposed as a peeled onion! But, no matter how fancy the desk, nor how fancy the title, remember he puts his pants on the same way you do every morning—one leg at a time!

Do your homework: By that we mean ask around (friends, business contacts, accountants, lawyers) and learn everything you can about the bank and its loan officer *before* you go in to make a formal loan application. Learn what their preferences are, what criteria for loans they emphasize, what business or personal contacts you have in common, their likes and dislikes (both personal and business). Put another way: If you were hot to get a job with a certain company, wouldn't you find out everything about the company's likes and dislikes in order to ingratiate yourself? Approach your bank loan visit the same way and chances are you'll soon have the bank unlocking their vaults in order to loan you the money you need.

HINT: Before you make your bank visit, make some notes on a piece of paper and bring it with you to cue yourself as to what to say (such as the purpose of the loan, how you plan to pay it back, what charge cards or charge accounts you have, and so on). After all, if you forget to bring out some favorable point at your meeting and then remember it when you're driving away, you'll have missed striking while the iron is hot.

Make a practice run: When you get a blank loan application, ask the bank to tell you everything that they'll want to know about you and bring a paper and pencil with you to make detailed notes. If you're not 100 percent clear about something that they'll want to know, do not hesitate to ask them to clarify it. It's better to ask for a further explanation at this early stage than to risk giving the bank an incorrect or incomplete loan application.

If you follow the advice outlined, do all your homework, and couple it with a favorable track record of loan repayment, chances are you'll get your loan and will be one giant step closer to owning the home you've got your eye on.

HOW TO USE COLLATERALIZED LOANS TO HELP BUY YOUR HOME

We've talked about different kinds of assets you might have that you would list on your personal financial statement when you apply for a personal loan at a bank. These assets can be used to secure a personal loan.

A signature loan is backed only by the bank's trust in you personally to repay your loan. A collateralized loan, which is backed by personal assets, has the following advantages:

1. You'll usually get your money quicker from the bank.

2. You'll usually get more favorable terms. When financial people use the word *term* in relation to a loan, be it a personal loan or a mortgage loan, they mean the length of time of the loan. This additional time might be helpful to you.

3. Because a collateralized loan is less risky to a lender than a signature loan, your rate of interest on the loan will be lower. How much lower depends on the money conditions at the time, the philosophy of the lending bank, and whether the collateral you offer is liquid (that is, something that can be turned into cash in a few days, such as stocks, bonds, or cash savings programs) or nonliquid (such as real estate or collectibles), plus the bank's evaluation of the quality of this asset. For example, the bank will look more favorably on stock collateral if it's of a major corporation listed on the New York or American Stock Exchange selling at over $10 than on stock in a small, nonlisted, over-the-counter company selling for under $10. In the first case,

the bank might extend your collateralized loan on 70 to 80 percent of the current market value of the stock. Thus if you owned $5,000 worth of IBM stock, they'd loan you, on a collateralized basis, $3,500. In the latter example they might extend you a collateralized loan on 50 percent or less of the current market value of the stock, depending on how actively the stock was traded, the company's overall financial standing, and other factors.

If you pledge an asset like stocks or bonds or other similar income-producing holdings as collateral for your loan, you'll still continue to receive the income from it even though the bank would hold the asset within its bank vaults until you have completed repayment on the loan. If you're fortunate enough to have this kind of asset to use to collateralize your loan, it's much to your benefit, because you continue to get the income from the asset and, at the same time, you'll be putting the asset to work rather than leaving it rest as a "passive" asset.

Besides banks, other kinds of lenders will evaluate assets you have for possible loan-pledging purposes. As an example, the Provident Loan Society of New York, 346 Park Avenue South, New York, NY 10010 makes loans against tangibles, such as diamonds, gold jewelry, silver, U.S. stamps, and coins. Also, S. H. Engel & Co. Inc., 38 Park Row, New York, NY 10038 makes pledge loans on stamp or philatelic properties. Firms such as these usually advertise in financial publications such as the *Wall Street Journal* or the financial sections of leading metropolitan newspapers in the Sunday editions.

USING COLLATERAL WHEN YOU DON'T HAVE COLLATERAL

A real estate investor friend of mine in San Antonio says it best: "When financially you're a mouse, go rent an elephant." Translation: When you don't have the cash—or the assets—go borrow them from someone else who does. To put this theory to work, find someone (a relative, a friend, a business or social contact, your attorney, doctor, employer) who owns stocks or bonds. Approach him on the basis that you want to rent his assets for a period of time (as long as the length of the loan you'd be getting at the bank) and would be willing to pay him for the loan. Obviously, you'd have to pay a rental fee for the use of holdings, and the amount of the fee (probably between 2-to-5 percentage points) would be dependent on your relationship with the other party, how safe the lending party felt his rented collateral would be in light of your reliability and trustworthiness, and on how long you'd need to rent the collateral. For example, let's say you approached your accountant to rent $10,000 worth of bonds out of the total bond portfolio he held. Knowing you to be reliable, he might rent them to you for, say, 4 percent per year for a two-year period. From his end he'd be getting an additional 4 percent yield on his bonds over and above the yield he currently enjoys, and you (for an annual cost of $400) would be getting $10,000 worth of bonds to take to a bank to pledge toward a collateralized loan. Always get a lawyer to draw up the appropriate papers in a transaction such as this.

This kind of transaction, with benefits for both parties, is being done more in today's tight money financial market where creativity has become the watchword.

Frankly, when you don't have the cash, then you have to be both creative and clever and have to learn how to capitalize on your character's plusses—as with the case of unsecured signature loans based on your character and your loan-repayment track record. If banks talk about the four C's (Cash, Character, Capacity, Collateral), perhaps the slogan for determined but cash-shy home buyers should be the three C's: Creativity, Capacity and Character.

ADDITIONAL LOAN SOURCES

Below is a partial list of some other sources of loanable funds offering unsecured loans up to $15,000 or more. These are usually referred to as Executive Loans by Mail, since all transactions are handled through the mail. The conditions insofar as how much your annual earnings must be, length and interest rate of loan, insurance requirements, and so on will vary from company to company, so write for their literature if you want to consider their loan program:

- Capital Financial Services
  1930 South Hill Street, Suite 208
  Oceanside, CA 92054

- Nationwide Finance Corporation
  1660 South Albion Street, Suite 927
  Denver, CO 80222

- Dial Financial Corporation
  2007 South Main Street
  P.O. Box 2321
  Santa Ana, CA 92707

- Executive Loan Service
  Suite 404
  Stemmons Tower West
  Dallas, TX 75207

- Postal Thrift Loans Incorporated
  703 Douglas Street
  Sioux City, IA

- ITT Credit Reserve
  2470 First Security Building
  Salt Lake City, UT

If you're interested in speed (the loan arrangements usually take approximately two to three weeks), confidentiality (these firms send their material to you in unmarked envelopes and don't go into detail as to loan purposes as banks do), and simplicity, these lenders, who advertise in financial newspapers and publications, might be helpful to you if you're able to handle the loan repayment schedule and interest charges. The big thing for you to keep in mind here, as with all the borrowing sources indicated in this book, is your ability to make proper loan repayments on schedule. We'll have much more to say about this aspect of borrowing in the closing section of this chapter.

ADDITIONAL FINANCING IDEAS: CO-SIGNER LOANS, READY RESERVE LOANS, CHARGE-CARD LOANS

If the bank requires a co-signer, that is, an individual the bank would go to for repayment in case you failed or were unable to repay, your most likely sources for a cooperative co-signer would probably be a member of your family, a friend, or a business contact. Failing this, you could rent a co-signer. In essence, you're renting financial strength. Remember, "If you're a mouse, go rent an elephant." Sunday editions of metropolitan newspapers and financial or business publications carry advertisements of individuals or firms willing to sign as co-signers for a fee, which might run from 1 to 5 percent of the loan amount; sometimes you'll see advertisements of financial finders who, for a fee of approximately 2 to 3 percent, can put you in contact with a co-signer. Think twice if your total combined charges for financial funder or co-signer are running you 5 or 6 percent or over, because these charges are *in addition* to the interest cost of the loan that the bank or other lender will be charging you.

Renting money is expensive and everything is certainly a lot more fun—and easier—when you have the cash and you don't have to go out in the cold world of commercial borrowing to look for funds. *Your best bet in the long run is to do as much of your borrowing from the home seller (which Chapters Two and Three cover in detail) rather than these other commercial sources.*

The primary reason for this is that the home seller's *primary* concern is disposing of his home, and therefore, when he's willing to work with you on some kind of financing arrangement, it's only as a means to an end (that is, in order to sell his house). Because of this, you'll invariably be able to work out *better* financial conditions with the home seller in terms of financing than with commercial lenders. In contrast, the banks, savings and loans, bank-by-mail concerns, overdraft loans, and other commercial lenders have as their primary objective making high-yielding and safe loans for themselves. In a word, the house seller is more *motivated* to give you better terms than a commercial lender because he *wants* to sell his home, a point you should keep in mind.

OTHER LOAN SOURCES

OVERDRAFT CHECKING

Different banks have different names for this kind of loan. They're called Cash Reserve, Check-O-Draft, Instant Cash, Checking Plus, for example. They are basically lines of credit (meaning that the bank thinks you're credit-worthy) that the bank is willing to extend. Once a bank has qualified you for their particular overdraft checking program, you can write checks beyond what you have in your account, up to the amount for which the bank feels you qualify. You'll be able to borrow from $500 to upwards of $10,000 this way; exactly how much will depend on the bank's policy on its overdraft checking program as it relates to their loan policies, to their competition, and to the extent of your overall financial credit worthiness.

You can get your funds rapidly with this kind of loan program and with a high degree of privacy. No one will ask you the purpose of your overdraft loan, as they would with a personal bank loan, where you are requested to indicate the purpose for the loan. Once your creditability has been established with the bank, then, this kind of overdraft checking program means your borrowed funds are available on a demand basis and can be used for any purpose.

It might pay you to check out the overdraft checking programs offered by different banks in your area and then decide on the one that could give you the most favorable arrangement. You might even want to set up an overdraft checking account with more than one bank, thereby diversifying your borrowing sources and spreading out your financial lines of credit.

CREDIT-CARD CHECKS

This loan program is similar to overdraft checking but is offered by bank credit cards, such as Master Charge. Bank credit card companies will offer you their own checks to use and, as with the bank overdraft checking account, will let you write checks up to the level to which they feel your overall financial position can qualify. Like bank programs, credit-card checks are quick and confidential, although limited in the amount of dollars they will extend.

CREDIT UNION

If you are a member of a credit union where you work, or if you are able to join one, it may pay you to check out their loan program, as they will extend short-term loans at generally competitive rates.

CONVENTIONAL BORROWING: A GREAT TOOL IF YOU CAN HANDLE IT

The last thing I'd want on my conscience is stimulating you to borrow money if you haven't prepared yourself for the responsibility borrowed funds entail. To me, preparing means you have laid the financial foundation of your life in other important areas as well.

First, you should have an adequate accident and health

insurance program and reasonably reliable, steady income sources to pay the premiums. Can you imagine the mess you'd be in with *no* accident and health insurance if you got injured, couldn't work, lost your income, yet were faced with both increasing medical bills *and* loan repayments that had to be met for money you had borrowed?

Second, you should have a good major medical insurance program for yourself and your family. Think of this: perhaps you can handle the $500 to $3,500 medical bills without help, but if you were suddenly hit with $10,000, $20,000, $30,000, or more in medical bills (it can happen no matter what your age or current health condition) *plus* trying to make loan repayments, you might soon find yourself in the bankruptcy court.

Third, you should have at your disposal some kind of cash reserve for unforeseen emergencies. I can't tell you how much cash it should be because I don't know how you live, but I feel it certainly ought to be enough to carry you for several months in case your major source of income ceased.

Fourth, you should have a fairly steady income with the prospects that this income source will be available to you for the foreseeable future. Don't borrow $10,000 today knowing there's a 50/50 chance that next month you'll be out of a job and out of the needed dollars to make your loan repayments.

Adequate insurance, some emergency cash, a steady job—I think these are primary prerequisites you *must* and *should* have *before* you even begin to think of borrowing funds for a home. I can't help but wonder if in our mad rush to buy things these days, we lose sight of the necessity of these important cornerstones to our financial well-being, and forget that we must have a fair amount of assurance that we'll have an adequate income

33

in the foreseeable future to cover loan repayments plus inflationary increases in the cost of our living.

It's fun—and easy—to walk into a bank, sign a loan paper, and walk out with $5,000, $10,000, $15,000, $20,000. The hard part comes later when you have to make those steady, relentless, and seemingly endless repayments. As they say in TV police programs: Don't do the crime if you can't do the time.

I hope in this chapter I've stimulated your thinking a little by exposing you to all the different techniques, areas, and approaches at your disposal that you can use to increase your cash so that you can go forward and buy your dream house. I trust I have made you aware that you have to prepare yourself for the loan process by having other parts of your "house in order": adequate emergency insurance programs, emergency cash, and the anticipated funds to repay your loans, and that you will have programmed yourself not to spend or depend on future pay increases until they become a reality.

All these loan techniques, and the preparation for them, are going to take time. Perhaps now you'll begin to see why in the beginning of the chapter I indicated you might need as much as four to six months to do all your financial homework before you ran around and got emotionally turned on by a lot of cute houses. In the following chapters I'll be showing you dozens of creative financing techniques and dollar-stretching techniques pointed toward one thing: showing you the financial way to buy that house!

CHAPTER TWO

CREATIVE FINANCING

Creative financing in residential real estate has, at long last, come into its own. Born out of necessity in the late 1970's and coming into full-blown acceptance in the 80's, creative financing offers the potential home buyer the financial techniques that can lead to home ownership. In the mid to late 70's, when loan interest rates and, more specifically, home mortgage rates coupled with increasing property prices began to become prohibitive, thousands of interested home buyers could no longer afford the cost of conventional mortgage money and had to abandon their hopes for home ownership, even though they had diligently saved and worked toward this goal. This sorry set of circumstances has had adverse repercussions throughout our country at many economic levels. Slackened home-buying activity not only has adversely affected mortgage activity but has taken a serious toll on the profitability of the real estate, building, banking, and home furnishings industries plus a host of other collateral industries. Because of the high mortgage rates from traditional mortgage sources, which were only reflecting the higher costs of money they in turn had to pay for, other sources for funds started to come into their own. All these other sources of money have come to be lumped together under the term "creative financing" and have several things in common:

First, most of these creative financing techniques bring the seller more into the picture in financing the home sale. Before creative real estate financing in residential property came into its own, a seller merely had to wait until a buyer with sufficient cash and an affordable mortgage in hand came along to buy the property. However, today it's a different story. It's the wise home seller who realizes that if he wants to increase his chances of selling his house within a reasonable time, he must familiarize himself with these techniques. Some form of owner financing plays an important role in many of these creative financing techniques; therefore the smart seller makes himself knowledgeable so that if and when the buyer or his broker presents any of these techniques as part of the financial structuring of the purchase, the seller will know what to do to take advantage of the offer.

Creative financing techniques are not new. They have been around for years in the real estate industry, where they have stood the test of time and proven their effectiveness in the real estate market. Most of them come out of the world of commercial real estate and are just now being modified to fit the needs of the single-family home market.

For years, small and large real estate investors, whether they were buying small apartment houses, residential rental properties (such as two-, three-, or four-family houses) or major income-producing complexes (such as large apartment houses and shopping centers) have successfully used many of these creative financing techniques to put their deals together.

They work most effectively when you, your broker, and your real estate lawyer have made yourselves knowledgeable about all their plusses and pitfalls. It helps when you are dealing with a seller who is interested and motivated to sell his property and who has become familiar with these techniques. (We'll have more to say about motivated sellers later.)

The element of time is a factor. As a buyer, you will have to give yourself ample time to learn these techniques and to find a broker or real estate lawyer who has learned them also—one who possesses the ability to educate the seller to their benefits and show him they are a practical and realistic way to sell his house. The fact that wise real estate brokers and sellers are making themselves increasingly knowledgeable about these techniques will speed up your home-buying goals and make them that much more attainable. Time also plays another role in creative financing, for many of these techniques offer a means whereby the buyer can *defer* payment to a later date.

Not every one of these techniques will be suitable for everyone in every home-buying situation. First, both you and the seller will have to feel comfortable with a given technique. A knowledgeable real estate broker, lawyer, or accountant can be an invaluable sounding board for you to discuss a given technique as it relates to a specific property you're interested in. Then, too, if one of these techniques is not acceptable to your seller, another one might suit his needs just as well. In other words, you'll want to remain flexible in your approach to these different techniques and modify a given technique, to fit the needs of the seller if you are to consummate a purchase of a home.

In the 80's, creative financing in real estate, properly used, can now offer you the means to buy your own home. Let's look into some of these alternative financing approaches that will partially circumvent or defer the current high-cost conventional financing or soften the impact of high money rates and high home prices.

ASSUMABLE MORTGAGES

A dream come true of any home buyer would be to find a low-interest assumable mortgage on a desired house that is for sale. The key words in that sentence, of course, are *assumable* and *low-interest*. An assumable mortgage would mean that you would be able to take over the existing mortgage intact, with the same interest rate, terms, and conditions that the current home owner now has. The obvious advantage is that if this mortgage was placed against the house many years ago by the current owner, its assumable interest rate (perhaps somewhere in the 5 to 9 percent range) would be *dramatically below* what *current* interest rates are. As of the early 1980's, single-family, owner-occupied mortgage interest rates are between 16 and 17 percent. No one knows what they'll be eventually. However, you can be certain that it's unlikely that you and I will ever again see single-digit mortgage interest rates offered by conventional mortgage sources. Those kinds of interest rates went out with cheap gasoline, inexpensive electricity, and the $2 haircut. However, if you were born under a four-leaf clover and, miracles upon miracles, you *found* a home for sale with an assumable low-interest mortgage, you'd be well advised to check on three things:

1. Although the property is offered for sale with an assumable mortgage, before you get yourself all excited, make sure that the broker selling the house or your real estate attorney reads the seller's actual mortgage document to make sure that it actually is an assumable mortgage.

2. Make sure that if title is transferred to you as the new owner, the bank that holds the assumable mortgage cannot charge you with an assumption charge at the closing. An assumption charge would be a predetermined amount of money which, from the bank's point of view, would help to compensate it for the fact that you'd be taking over an existing mortgage at a rate that is substantially lower than the current rate on mortgages.

3. The assumable mortgage should not have a certain type of acceleration clause, sometimes referred to as a "due-on-sale" clause. This clause would mean that in the event that title to the house was transferred to someone else, the remaining current balance on the mortgage would become due and payable. This, of course, would completely defeat your purpose in taking over an assumable mortgage in the first place.

As you can see, this is no area for an amateur, so get yourself a competent real estate lawyer to read the seller's mortgage papers. In fact, any time you make an offer for any property, you should make your offer subject to three things:

1. *Subject to satisfactory financing*: This clause would protect you because you would not have to go through with the purchase unless all the financing comes through the way you want. Don't let a house's charming fireplace or a panoramic view saddle you with unsatisfac-

tory financing that's going to choke you; otherwise, your dream house will turn into a scream house!

2. *Subject to satisfactory licensed inspection*: You'll want to find out about the house's wiring, plumbing, structure, foundation, roof, septic and water system *before* you actually buy it, not *after*. If you find problems *before* you buy, you might get the seller to adjust the price or conditions of sale. If you discover problems *after* you've bought the house, you'll wind up poorer.

3. *Subject to advice of counsel*: You'll want a lawyer to look at all documents on record that pertain to the house: whether it's a possible assumable mortgage as mentioned, whether there are liens or troublesome easements on the property, whether there's a clear title to the property, and so on. The seller too will be working with the help of his real estate lawyer to check on potential pitfalls. One of the most important of these is that the seller would not continue to be held responsible for the mortgage in the event that the new owner defaulted on the payments. Some may call this "subject to advice of counsel" a Weasel clause, but I call it a "back-door" clause. If you really needed the use of it and couldn't go through with the purchase, you'd call it a blessing!

Your assumable mortgage, clear of any of the kinds of problems referred to, would certainly offer you an excellent opportunity to buy a home with financing in an affordable range. Unfortunately, these properties with low-interest assumable mortgages are snapped up quicker than a two-for-one bread sale at your local food market and, in most cases, they don't even make the newspaper listings. Then, too, sellers with low-rate assumable mortgages are no dummies. They know that they've got something good and therefore they'll probably be looking for a higher price on their property.

This brings us to a basic concept. If you want to approach this area of buying a home from a professional point of view as a professional real estate investor would, keep this in mind: *The way you structure the financing should be more important to you than the price you pay for the property*. That may sound strange but it's basic to the success that real estate investors enjoy when they're buying property using leverage techniques that use little or none of their own cash. If you can get the financing you want, then the price of the property should be secondary. *In other words, if the seller lets you buy under your conditions of financing, then you in turn should be willing to make some concessions in price.*

Unfortunately, most people in their negotiations get all hung up on the price of the property rather than getting favorable financing terms. When I buy a property, I'll sometimes tell the broker that I'll buy either of two ways: the seller's price and my terms or my price and the seller's terms. Realistically, it will be tough for you as a buyer (or a seller) to get it 100 percent in both areas. Therefore, as a cash-shy buyer, you would be best to shoot for getting favorable financing terms, techniques, and conditions in exchange for the seller's offering price.

Many of these assumable mortgages are VA (Veterans Administration) or FHA (Federal Housing Authority) mortgages which have been written years before by local lending banks and insured by these federal agencies, thereby allowing the bank to offer a lower interest rate because the risk element has been reduced. These VA and FHA assumable mortgages are also low-rate mortgages and could be just what you need in order to afford a home. Your best chance of getting these mort-

41

gages would be in older, more settled neighborhoods. If you don't have to live in a specific town then here's a hint for finding such homes. Get a map of your state. Ask knowledgeable people (that is, police departments, real estate brokers, bankers) to find out the names of any Armed Forces Installations within the state. Draw a 25- to 50-mile circle on your map around each of these Armed Forces camps and then contact every real estate broker in that area. Inasmuch as these VA assumable loans (which usually required little cash down) would have been put on homes that were built to satisfy the needs of Army personnel families, tell the real estate broker that you want to see any VA or FHA assumable mortgage houses as they come on the market. If you really pursue these brokers in a persistent but pleasant manner, the vast majority will work hard for you. Be polite and considerate on the telephone, keep appointments promptly, phone to cancel dates you can't keep, and write a gracious thank you note for time spent on your behalf. If you follow this tack, chances are you'll soon be seeing houses with assumable mortgages that carry mortgage interest rates you can live with.

This house may or may not be *exactly* what you had in mind but if it gets you into home ownership then at least it's got you on the house-ownership track. At a later date, when you've got some equity in this house, you can sell it and move on to another home more to your liking.

LAND CONTRACT (ALSO CALLED CONTRACT OF SALE OR CONTRACT FOR DEED)

In times of high-interest mortgage rates, sellers have trouble selling their property and buyers have trouble qualifying for affordable mortgage money. This dual problem has helped to stimulate more interest in the conveyance of property under an agreement referred to as a land contract. If, for example, a home owner has an existing 10 percent mortgage on his house and a potential buyer would have to pay an unacceptable 15 percent for a new mortgage, the desired goal would be to allow the buyer to avail himself of this seller's existing 10 percent mortgage. It is this interest in trying to utilize the existing lower interest rate that has popularized the use of land contract technique.

Under this arrangement, the buyer, who would be the equitable owner and have full rights of possession of the property, would make monthly payments to the seller (or to a third party escrow account), who, in turn, would continue to make his payments on his 10 percent mortgage while still holding title to the property. Eventual title to the house would pass to the buyer only after he had made a certain amount of mortgage payments or was able to acquire an acceptable new first mortgage. Needless to say, this kind of sophisticated arrangement should be entered into only with the help of a competent real estate lawyer, as there are pitfalls that would have to be provided for. To name only one, the seller's own 10 percent mortgage document should not include a due-on-sale clause or acceleration clause. As was mentioned in the preceding section, this clause states that if the title passes to a new owner, then the entire remaining balance of the mortgage becomes due and payable. The land contract agreement endeavors to circumvent this possibility since actual title to the property remains with the seller and only the *use* of the property has been transferred to the buyer. However, different mortgaging banks in different states have interpreted this due-on-sale clause differently and some have challenged, with varying degrees of success, the use of the land contract agreement. Therefore, it is best to get a local real estate attorney's opinion as to both the content of the seller's mortgage and the way the bank that held the seller's mortgage might react to the use of a land contract agreement in the transaction. A good attorney will also be able to set up the mechanics of monthly mortgage payments.

With the land contract agreement, time is saved because you're avoiding deed registration and appropriate financial approval. Thus, for a buyer with possibly more character than cash at his disposal this is a quick and creative way to utilize a lower-interest-rate mortgage that is already in place. The land contract agreement, where and when feasible, with professional legal advice, has come into its own in the 80's and has now opened up a means by which thousands of people have been able to enjoy the benefits of home ownership. In your search for home-buying techniques, you'd be well advised to look into all aspects of the land contract agreement.

MORTGAGE SUBSIDY (SOMETIMES CALLED MORTGAGE BUY-DOWN)

Another technique whereby the seller is participating in the transaction is mortgage subsidy. A real estate investor friend of mine used it with his sale of an eleven-unit apartment house. When he put this rental property on the market, mortgage interest rates were quite high. The property remained unsold for approximately a year. The costly mortgage money was discouraging prospective investor-buyers when they reviewed the property's gross rental income and expenses, added the high cost of mortgage money, and considered the resultant net return. The listing broker, a creative realtor with a keane (sic) sense of financing, suggested a newer approach. He suggested that the seller pay the buyer an amount of money in order to offset the inordinately high mortgage interest costs and thereby bring down to a more acceptable range the actual effective cost of the mortgage. The seller was willing to consider the concept and the broker shortly found a buyer. The transaction went as follows: The asking price of the property was $200,000. The buyer was to get a first mortgage of $150,000 at a rate of 16 percent; the remaining $50,000 was to come from the buyer's cash down and a second mortgage from the seller. At that rate, the investment had only limited interest to the buyer. The broker suggested that the seller pay the buyer a 2 percent mortgage subsidy fee for the first year (2 percent of a $150,000 first mortgage = $3,000) and a 1 percent mortgage subsidy fee for the second year ($1,500). With these payments from seller to buyer to help offset the excessively high interest rates, the "numbers" on the property became that much more attractive and, as a result, a deal was put together.

Thanks to the creative thinking of the broker, the seller was able to sell his property even during a high-interest period and walk away with a nice profit, even after paying the mortgage subsidy fee to the buyer. The buyer was satisfied with the return on his investment given the mortgage subsidy setup. And, looking down the road, the buyer knew that he'd be able to get his property's rent roll increased enough so that when the third year rolled around he'd be able to handle the mortgage payments without the seller's offsetting mortgage subsidy payments. (Builders and sellers of condominiums refer to this mortgage subsidy technique as a "buy-down" provision.)

During high mortgage interest rate periods when sellers are having difficulty selling their property, this technique offers you the opportunity to purchase a home while serving your needs as well as the needs of the seller. If you use this technique as a buyer, you must be fairly well assured that you will be able to handle the full mortgage payments once the seller's subsidy payments cease and that you *might* be able to get a new and *lower* rated mortgage at a future time, although I wouldn't hold my breath on that one.

WRAPAROUND MORTGAGE (ALSO CALLED ALL-INCLUSIVE DEED OF TRUST)

Here's a fancy sounding financing technique that comes right out of the world of commercial real estate and, fortunately, can be usable in the single-family market, under the guidance of a real estate lawyer. It's the kind of technique that sounds more complicated than it really is, so don't be frightened by its sophisticated-sounding razzmatazz.

The wraparound mortgage concept comes into being where there is a low-interest mortgage already extant on a property. In order to avoid the need to secure a new high-interest mortgage (assuming the buyer could qualify and afford it), the seller creates a new mortgage himself at a rate lower than the current rates. In a sense, he becomes the lender. The higher current rate mortgage wraps around the existing lower-rated mortgage against the property. In a sense, the buyer makes mortgage payments to the seller who in turn continues to make payments on the underlying mortgage. For example, Mr. and Mrs. Home Seller, with a $100,000 home for sale, have an existing $30,000 mortgage at 9 percent interest. The prospective buyer can come up with only $10,000 cash (not the $20,000 to $25,000 cash the bank would require) and he cannot qualify with the bank for the current 17½ percent mortgage interest rates offered. At this point, a wraparound mortgage could possibly come into play. The seller takes a $10,000 down payment and has a second trust deed, subject to state laws, prepared for the remaining $90,000, which he offers to the buyer at 13 percent (or whatever rate he sets, that would be lower than the current rates from banks yet higher than his home's current mortgage rate of 9 percent). Under this arrangement, the old 9 percent mortgage has *not* been paid off and a new mortgage has been written which simply "wraps" around it. The buyer makes his monthly payments to the seller, based on the terms of this new mortgage of $90,000 with interest at 13 percent. The seller continues making payments to the first lender on the $30,000 that he still owes at 9 percent, and, since he's charging his buyer 13 percent on the entire $90,000 amount, he is netting himself 4 percent on $30,000 and 13 percent on the remaining $60,000 of this wrap mortgage. The difference between a land contract and a wraparound mortgage is that with the land contract the actual legal title remains with the seller and equitable title resides with the buyer. In the wraparound mortgage, legal title is conveyed to the buyer and an equitable interest through the wraparound mortgage is retained by the seller. Note, however, that on the wraparound mortgage situation, the transfer of legal title may activate a due on sale clause contained in the first mortgage. A competent real estate attorney should be consulted to review the documents and advise you.

Under this wraparound mortgage arrangement the buyer is able to buy with a lower cash down payment and also is charged an overall mortgage interest rate that is lower than prevailing rates. In this example, the buyer would be charged 13 percent by the seller's wraparound mortgage, certainly lower than the prevailing rate of 17½ percent. For the seller, the wraparound mortgage offers a technique to sell his property during high-interest rate periods when prospective buyers would normally be knocked out of the box because of their financial inability to handle the monthly mortgage payments. He would probably structure the mortgage as a 25- or 30-year pay-out and with a balloon payoff somewhere. The seller is also making a good rate of return on his equity in the property (13 percent on his $60,000 equity) plus a little bit on the mortgage that he still owes (that is, he's paying 9 percent interest on his original $30,000 mortgage but receiving 13 percent from the seller, so he's picking up 4 percent interest for himself). In case of default, the seller could take the property back relatively simply under the second trust deed arrangement.

The wraparound mortgage technique has the same potential problems as the land contract technique. One is the possible enforceable due-on-sale clause that might exist in the home owner's primary mortgage. If the first lender has such a clause in his mortgage note, he might demand a full payoff at the time the home is sold. In some states the primary lenders are running into problems trying to enforce due-on-sale clauses because they have to be able to prove that the safety of their loan repayment is being jeopardized by the use of the new mortgage. This is all pretty hairy stuff and no one statement can be made that will apply equally to every property, all underlying mortgages, all lenders, or each interpretation. It behooves you to touch base with a local real estate lawyer and explore all aspects of these types of dealings.

There is another creative financing approach that could grow out of a wraparound mortgage. You might be able to sit down with the bank that holds the primary mortgage and work out a new *blended* interest rate that both you and the bank can live with. This kind of arrangement seems to be coming more into play. The buyer can take over the mortgage at a new blended rate (such as 13 percent in our wraparound example) that would be higher than the old rate (9 percent in our example) but lower than the prevailing high rates (17½ percent in our example). A local "on-the-ball" real estate broker would probably know if the local bank holding the mortgage would be interested to work out such an arrangement.

HINT: In this kind of arrangement your seller can possibly be of help. Get him to tell the mortgage bank that he'll keep part or all of the cash proceeds from the sale in an account at the bank if a mutually agreeable arrangement with the buyer can be worked out. Sometimes this can be the extra inducement for a bank to work out an arrangement, sweetened even more if the real estate broker also commits himself to keep part or all of his commissions in an account at the same bank. Banks continually need new deposits and if you can't bring them your own money (because you just don't have it), then you may be able to increase your chances of getting what you want by being instrumental in getting *other* interested parties to bring *their* money to the bank. Banks, particularly smaller banks, are usually open to negotiation, particularly if you have a good prior relationship with them, such as a strong real estate broker–banker relationship or funds that you could direct to a bank. Moral: Don't leave any stone unturned when you're trying to work out some kind of financial arrangement.

RENT WITH OPTION TO PURCHASE (SOMETIMES CALLED *LEASE-OPTION*)

Another creative financing technique that's finding a ready market these days is the rent-with-option-to-purchase approach. In this technique the buyer makes arrangements to rent a home at a mutually agreed upon price with an option to buy at some future date when, he hopes, mortgage interest rates will have come down. In such an agreement the renter will put up option money, possibly 10 to 20 percent of the purchase price, as a commitment to buy at a future price and time, which are also mutually agreed upon prior to his taking occupancy.

More and more homes are being offered under this kind of arrangement because erstwhile sellers realize that the market for qualified buyers shrinks as the mortgage interest rates escalate. Under a lease-purchase option, the option to purchase usually runs from 12 to 24 months, possibly longer. The home owner receives some minimal cash in the form of option money, which is usually nonrefundable, in exchange for a commitment to sell at a later date at a price agreed upon. To the home owner's advantage is the fact that he'll retain tax advantages since he is now a landlord and can qualify for depreciation on the building, which is now a rental income-producing piece of property. At the same time, he will receive monthly rental income from the renter/buyer, which usually is equal to the monthly mortgage payments he will be paying. Moreover, the arrangement offers the seller a means whereby he can move on to another location.

For the renter/buyer, this is a low-cost way to get into home occupancy. Initially the renter/buyer is paying only option money and the agreed-upon monthly rental. The buyer also might be able to get the owner to apply some of the rental payments as a credit toward the future price on the house. Depending on how pressed the home owner is to put this arrangement into writing, the buyer might be able to apply 50 to 75 percent of the rental payments toward the purchase of the house. However, like almost everything else in real estate this is up for negotiation. In real estate, what you don't ask for you don't get and that's the beauty of many of these creative financing techniques: they do not have a lot of the rigid rules and regulations normally experienced with conventional lending institutions. You are also on your own when you're putting these kinds of techniques together, and that is why it's particularly important to work with a real estate broker experienced in these matters or with a professional real estate consultant, as well as to hire the services of a competent real estate lawyer.

The lease with option to purchase agreement is a good technique. It gives the buyer and seller a mechanism to defer the closing on a home sale and transferring of its deed to a later time when mortgage rates might be lower. For the seller who is not in dire need of immediate substantial equity cash from his house, it furnishes a means whereby, if he has carefully checked both the references and credit rating of the renter/buyer, he can rent out his property and apply the income toward his own mortgage. Having set up this arrangement, he can then move on. For home owners who might be relocating and who would therefore want to offer their home with a fairly simple financing technique that could be explained readily to a large number of people, the lease with option to purchase might be just the ticket.

HINT: When you, as the buyer-to-be, discuss with the home owner the ultimate purchase price of the house, obviously you will probably be talking a lower sales figure than the seller. One of the best guidelines to try to arrive at a mutually agreeable price is to ascertain what the future percentage increase in local comparable properties might be for the length of time you're discussing. And if the seller is holding out for a little higher price than you feel you want to pay, you could come back to him and agree only if he's willing either to apply a higher amount of your monthly rental payments toward a credit against the purchase price, or to lower the money option amount, or to extend the length of the option period. A combination of any of these offers plenty of negotiating space. Your ability to get a good arrangement will depend on the strength of his desire to sell in combination with your ability to negotiate the best set of circumstances for yourself that you can. Make no mistake, your ability, or that of your real estate broker as negotiator on your behalf, will make a vast difference in your ability to get a good deal. (I'll have some suggestions in this area of effective negotiations later in the book.)

LAND LEASE TECHNIQUE

In certain parts of the country, most notably California and Hawaii, the concept of land leases is becoming another tool for creative financing to lower purchase costs. Under this kind of arrangement, the cost of the land is excluded from the purchase price. (However, the home purchaser is paying a lease fee for the underlying land.) By so doing, developers can reduce needed down payments from prospective purchasers and also reduce the monthly payments on the house itself by approximately 25 percent. These land lease arrangements are written for a long term, upwards of 99 years. A buyer would also want to see that an option to buy the land, certainly within a five-year period at an agreed-upon price, is part of the arrangement. It would make sense, as with the lease with option to buy technique, to see that as much as possible of the land rental fee is applicable to the eventual purchase price.

Builders seem to like land lease arrangements because they can sell the house for an operating profit and possibly retain the land for a favorable long-term capital gains transaction at a later date. Also, with the land not included in the total price, the property has a wider base of popular appeal and a better chance for prospective buyers to qualify for a mortgage loan. It is likely that the appeal and feasibility of the land lease arrangement will gain more acceptance as it comes into play in different areas of our country. Therefore it's advisable for you at least to be aware of the basic concept.

FIRST MORTGAGE FINANCING

You might, in your house-hunting expeditions, come across a home for sale that is free and clear of mortgage. This is usually an older home in an older neighborhood where the current owners, probably well along in years, have lived all their lives. If luck is with you, you might be able to arrange financing with the sellers holding the first mortgage substantially below the market rate if you, in turn, give them their price or close to it. In all likelihood, the sellers will not want to extend a long-term mortgage, so you might arrange a short term payoff called a balloon payment; in four, five, or six years you'd either have to pay off the mortgage or possibly renegotiate it in exchange for a long-term (25 to 30 years or more) *pay-out* which serves to lower your monthly mortgage payments. Or, you could try to find out what the sellers need to receive financially as a monthly mortgage income and work backwards, custom designing a mortgage that would fit both your needs. Remind them also that such a mortgage, collateralized by their home, would be excellent collateral if they in turn had need for immediate cash beyond any cash-down you would have to put up.

As with almost every real estate transaction, if you can find out what the needs of the *other* party are and structure your offer to encompass those needs, the seller will be amenable to at least trying to work toward your needs. Unfortunately, most people work just the reverse and try to satisfy their own needs first to the total exclusion of the other party. In so doing, they usually don't get what they could have achieved for themselves if they had taken another tack. As a cash-shy home buyer, you are, in a sense, the "seller" in that you want the home owner to "buy" your concept of deferred financing. In order to accomplish this in the financial structuring of your offer, you should find out the needs of the home owner and endeavor to satisfy them. For example, what is important to him may be an extra quick closing, or tax considerations, or cash-down needs versus long-term needs, or personal property to be kept or sold, or need for full price versus favorable financing for you, or a particular motivation for selling. Real estate is very much a people business. Train yourself to think in terms of people rather than property. Rest assured that if you satisfy the needs of the seller as a person, then you'll stand an excellent chance of getting the property. As a real estate friend of mine puts it, "People have to be *satisfied* before property changes hands. Buyers and sellers are people with needs; the property is only incidental to the transaction."

CREATIVE DOWN PAYMENTS

When it comes to a down payment toward a purchase, there's no law saying that all of your down payment has to be in cash. Cash, after all, is a medium to buy things of value, so if you have other items of value (that is, a boat, a car, collector's items, coins, valuables, land, antiques, a mortgage you hold, services you can render as a plumber, doctor, builder, electrician) then make them part of your down payment in lieu of cash or to supplement your cash down payment.

Also, when you make an offer with a cash down payment, there is no law that says the entire cash payment has to be paid, *in full*, at the *time of the closing*. A real estate friend of mine just bought a house with financing he felt would satisfy the seller's needs and his own cash-limited needs. He bought a $65,000 three-bedroom house with a down payment derived from a second mortgage of $21,000 he was holding on a small apartment house he had sold earlier, plus $5,000 cash, payable as follows: $1,000 at the closing, $2,000 on the first anniversary of the closing (at 9 percent interest), and $2,000 on the second anniversary of the closing. The balance of the purchase price, $39,000, my friend got from the seller in the form of a 72-month, interest only, purchase money mortgage, with a balloon payment for the full amount due in the 72nd month. (Prior to that my friend figured he would sell the property, trade it, or refinance it.) My friend had already arranged with the selling broker to pay a large part of his commission over a period of time, and therefore he did not need a lot of cash up front for that purpose. If, by the way, you have an excellent financial record and a spotless reputation, and if you can be instrumental in bringing several important listings or qualified buyers to him, the broker might loan you part of his commission upon the sale of the house to you (where permitted by state regulations). In difficult real estate times like these, some real estate brokers are in a position to have to take back a small note for a part of their commission (if the seller isn't getting enough cash out of the deal), or he might consider (don't hold your breath on this one) loaning some of his commission in order to see the transaction completed. More acceptable to a broker might

56

be the idea of his placing part of the commission due him in a certain bank if that could help the bank look with more favor at a pending mortgage situation the broker is involved with.

These, then, are some of the most common creative financing techniques that are coming to the forefront in the turbulent, high-interest-rate days of the 1980's. You don't have to be psychic to realize that the need for these financing techniques is an outgrowth of the needs of cash-shy home buyers fighting the prospect of escalating home prices and prohibitive mortgage carrying costs. These needs will increase over the foreseeable future, and because of the greater acceptance of these financing instruments, it will become increasingly easier for buyers, sellers, and brokers to utilize these techniques. The smart prospective buyer who learns all he can about dollar-stretching and creative financing techniques will be the one who will be able to buy a home now.

Conversely, if you plan to wait on the sidelines until conventional financing comes back into an acceptable range that fits your needs exactly, you might have a long wait with no assurance that at the end of it you'll be able to afford the higher home prices. A word to the wise is sufficient. Learn everything you can about the different techniques this book covers, discuss them in detail with realtors and real estate lawyers, and do the most important thing: buy that home for yourself!

CHAPTER THREE

HOW TO GET THE SELLER TO HELP YOU

The best technique for using as little of your own out-of-pocket cash as possible for a home will come from your ability to get the seller to take back a second mortgage. For the cash-shy home buyer the world of second mortgages is a dream come true! It is a made-to-order arrangement whereby, after the seller and buyer negotiate a purchase price both can live with, the seller then lends the buyer part of the total agreed-upon purchase price in the form of a second mortgage.

Here is a typical example: The seller agrees to sell his house for $60,000. This total price will come from the following sources:

Buyer's out-of-pocket cash:	$ 9,000
Buyer's first mortgage from a local lending institution:	$45,000
Second mortgage extended from the seller to the buyer:	$ 6,000
Total	$60,000

This kind of second mortgage is more accurately known as a "purchase money mortgage" because it is part of the total purchase price of the property. Sometimes brokers and sellers refer to this arrangement as "taking back paper," that is, the seller (the mortgagee) is taking back a mortgage note for a certain amount of money in lieu of actual cash from the buyer (the mortgagor). He will be paid back over a period of time under terms and conditions agreed upon by both parties.

When your needs and those of a seller can both be served by a financing tool such as a purchase money mortgage, then its use will grow in acceptance throughout the country. That is exactly what's happening in today's economy and it will be the case for decades to come. After all, the seller wants to sell his home and the buyer wants to buy. However, the major problem area that has hampered more buyers' and sellers' getting together to transfer ownership has been a meeting of the minds on the property's price and the buyer's ability to finance the purchase. Make no mistake, as the price of homes continues to rise, meeting those prices will become more of a problem. The use of financing tools such as the purchase money mortgage can help bridge the gap.

This development can mean several things in the future. As more sellers become aware of this financing tool, they will be more willing to extend second mortgages to the buyers. Furthermore, more brokers are becoming familiar with the fine points of the purchase money mortgage as a means of getting home sellers together with buyers. Also, more lawyers, lenders, accountants, and real estate consultants find themselves working with purchase money mortgages and are making themselves more knowledgeable about how they work.

As a cash-conscious home buyer, you derive several advantages from getting the seller to extend you a second mortgage. One of the biggest advantages is that the home seller himself is a ready-made source to help finance the purchase. His primary concern is to sell, and his extending a purchase money mortgage is a highly useful tool to accomplish that goal. Also, because the commercial lenders' primary concern is profits and safety, they will look for higher interest rates or more restrictive conditions on a second mortgage than the home seller. Moreover, the home seller who extends a purchase money mortgage will have a quicker sale on his property since he is supplying part of the financing.

Here is another example of how this technique can work to the advantage of both parties to the transaction. Bill and Barbara have their Baltimore house on the market because Bill is moving to California for a new career opportunity. But their $75,000 home has been on the market unsold for more months than they anticipated and they are beginning to panic. A previous offer on the property has fallen through because the prospective buyers did not have sufficient cash and the concept of a purchase money mortgage had not been introduced into the negotiations. The Smiths have been looking for a house in the area in the same general price range as Bill and Barbara's house. They make an offer of a $72,000 overall purchase price subject to their getting a satisfactory first mortgage of $54,000 from a local lending institution, a second mortgage for $10,000 from Bill and Barbara for a term of four years at an interest rate pegged to the lending institution's rate, and cash down of $8,000. Bill and Barbara, after getting a credit check on the Smiths from a local credit bureau and receiving advice from their attorney on the offer, accept, sell their home, and are able to move to California on schedule.

The use of the purchase money mortgage speeded up the sales process for the sellers and *time was a factor*. In sum, the use of a purchase money mortgage avoided the need for further selling time for the seller's house and it afforded the buyers a quick means to nail down the purchase of the home that they wanted.

Clearly, another advantage to the buyer is that the buyer will require the use of less of his own out-of-pocket cash to complete the purchase. Cash is, for most of us, a scarce commodity, and many times the use of a purchase money mortgage will make the difference between being able to buy a home or not. Even if the buyer has sufficient cash to make a full down payment without the use of a purchase money mortgage, he might find it advisable to hold more available cash in reserve for unanticipated emergencies rather than to commit it all. For example, let's say a buyer has the $10,000 cash needed to make a particular down payment and the seller is willing to take back a second mortgage of $3,000 for four years at 12 percent with interest only payments required annually and the full $3,000 payment due at the end of the period. A full principal payment coming such as this at the end of the mortgage period is called a balloon payment, and a mortgage where only interest payments are made is known as a standing mortgage. In this example, our buyer chooses not to have to commit his out-of-pocket $3,000 cash but would rather have the $3,000 to hold in liquid reserve for other purposes. However, he will have to come up with the $3,000 at the end of the third year to pay off his balloon mortgage payment to the seller.

Finally, a purchase money mortgage is going to keep the seller honest. If the seller has purposely made any claims about the property that are less than accurate, it will be advantageous for you to have purchased the property with a purchase money mortgage. The mere existence of a purchase money mortgage being held by a seller for funds still owed him by the buyer acts as a deterrent to the seller who might otherwise be tempted to shade the truth concerning important claims about the property.

In this connection, I recall the case of a friend who bought a three-bedroom home for investment purposes from a seller who was about to be foreclosed on the property. The total purchase price was $63,000, composed of $9,000 cash down, a first mortgage in the amount of $47,000, and a one-year standing mortgage from the seller for the balance in the amount of $7,000 at 12 percent. The contract of sale further stipulated that the seller could remain in the house for four weeks after the closing and at the end of four weeks the premises would have to be vacated and left "broom clean." When the four weeks passed and the seller vacated the property, he left a mess throughout the house—furniture, cartons, boxes, debris, and so forth. My friend had to hire costly extra help to clean it up. His cleanup costs ran well over $500, *but* he was able to have it deducted from the outstanding balance of the second mortgage principal owed the seller, thus reducing the size of the second mortgage debt and saving himself on the interest cost for the balance of the term of the debt. Moreover, he kept the seller honest by making him pay for his misfeasance.

In a nutshell, a purchase money mortgage can mean less out of pocket cash and generally more favorable conditions, such as a lower rate of interest or a more convenient pay-back schedule, as well as a quick, in-place source of needed financing to complete the purchase when time is a factor.

It's best to keep in mind that many home sellers are first-time sellers and may not be familiar with the concept of the purchase money mortgage. Therefore, it will be the wise broker or buyer who approaches this area of taking back a second mortgage slowly, making sure that the seller fully understands what the concept is and how it can serve their mutual needs.

HOW HOUSE BUYERS CAN GET RELUCTANT SELLERS TO "TAKE BACK PAPER"

One of the best things you can do as a cash-shy buyer is to find out as much as you can about your seller and his selling motivations. This is knowledge that you can turn to your advantage. Is he relocating? Moving to a smaller or a larger home? A new job? Is there a business or marriage split-up? There are a host of reasons why people sell their houses, some of which put the seller under pressure which can work to the buyer's goals.

In the previous example of the buyer who bought the three-bedroom home from the messy home owner, the purchaser well understood the importance of doing his homework. In that case, the buyer knew that the owner was in danger of losing his property to his mortgaging bank. My friend reasoned that the element of time would be the biggest motivating factor; so, he therefore gave the seller an early closing so that his property would not be taken away and gave him the price he wanted, but he made the purchase subject to a purchase money mortgage, thereby using less of his own out-of-pocket cash.

Learning the seller's reasons for selling, either through

the broker or through discreet inquiry in the community, may well reveal the real motivation behind the sale and could lead you into finding a receptive audience for a purchase funded in part by a purchase money mortgage.

One real estate broker I know showed a prospective home buyer a house for sale by an elderly couple. When the prospective buyer first visited the house with the realtor, he sensed that the wife was not looking forward to spending the cold winter in the house. Once back at the broker's office, he suggested that the broker introduce the subject of warmer climate and Florida living to the couple. The broker, who knew some Florida realtors, was able to stimulate the seller's interest in the idea of Florida living and, at the appropriate time, he followed through with an offer from the cash-shy buyer to buy their property, subject to a purchase money mortgage that was agreeable to both parties.

In both of these cases, the cash-shy buyers were able to get their sellers involved with a purchase money mortgage because they had taken the time to understand the motivations of the sellers and acted on what they had learned so that they could get what they wanted.

Therefore, as a buyer, it is wise to keep your eyes and ears open for motivation clues. A chance remark, a passing comment from the seller, a neighbor or a friend might just supply you with some valuable insight that could help buy the home you want at the lowest price and with the least amount of out-of-pocket cash!

The cash-shy buyer and his broker should be sure to point out to a home seller several points of possible benefit of taking a purchase money mortgage.

With the continuing depreciation of the dollar's purchasing power, the element of time becomes an important tool for a buyer. Clearly, the use of a purchase money mortgage will make for a quicker sale because the seller is supplying part of the financing. In so doing, the seller is getting much of his equity out of the property that much quicker. In these days of depreciating dollars, he would then have liquid dollars to put into whatever high-yielding money-market instruments he chose. Remember that most home sellers are usually impatient to sell their property, and this kind of home seller is usually amenable to some kind of second mortgage because it offers them a tool to make the sale.

Usually a reluctant home seller will be won over on the idea of taking back a second mortgage if he is made aware of the fact that he stands a better chance of getting a better price for his property than if all the needed up-front cash had to come from the buyer. This is an understandable trade-off; after all, if the seller is willing to supply some of the financing for the property's purchase, then it is not unrealistic for him to look to the buyer for a fuller price in exchange. At the same time, for the cash-shy home buyer the higher price will probably still be advantageous because it gives him the means to buy the house. Look at it this way: If you, as the cash-shy buyer, saw a house you want selling for $60,000 but were short of the up-front cash, your choices might boil down to these:

1. Pay the full price, or whatever you could negotiate. For example, a house offered at $60,000 might be negotiated to a $57,000 purchase price with 15 percent cash down of $8,550, subject to a satisfactory first mortgage from a lending institution of $42,750 (75 percent) and a four-year purchase money mortgage of $5,700 from the seller (10 percent of purchase price) with interest rate the same (or slightly higher) than that of the lending institution.

2. In contrast, a lower than $57,000 price might prevail to the buyer who had the needed 25 percent cash down available ($14,250) to consummate a sale, with the balance (75 percent) of the purchase price still coming from a lending institution. For example, let's say the price is negotiated down 10 percent less than $60,000, or $54,000. If cash were no problem, then you'd have to come up with $13,500 (25 percent of $54,000), and obtain the balance of $40,500 (75 percent of $54,000) from a lending institution.

Which would you prefer? In case number 1 you would pay a fuller price ($57,000) but only $8,550 cash up front. In case 2, if you had the cash, which you probably don't, you'd be buying at $54,000 but you'd have to come up with $13,500!

When you've found a house you like, *buy it*—even if you have to borrow some of the money from the seller to do it and possibly, but not necessarily, pay a little more for it. Think of it this way: In the last analysis, your home purchase will probably prove to be one of the best all-around financial investments you'll ever make, and four years from now your home's value will probably have increased *more* than what you'll owe on the second mortgage; you'll also be paying back with cheaper dollars; and you'll have a house and all the psychic returns in pleasure associated with home ownership.

The cash-shy buyer, or his broker, might further stimulate a seller's interest in taking back a second mortgage because this method of sale might be more advantageous to the seller from a tax point of view. Each home sale is unique and each seller's needs (a quicker sale, a higher priced sale, or a better tax-related sale) all become points of consideration.

Most important, there is a market for second mortgages that the home seller/mortgage holder can sell to!

Most active real estate brokers know many individuals (accountants, lawyers, investors, and the like) who are interested in buying, at a discount, a second mortgage that has a single-family house as collateral, inasmuch as this is usually considered a fairly safe investment. For example, Mr. and Mrs. White, in order to complete the sale of their $60,000 home, take back a three-year second mortgage for $6,000 from the buyers, Mr. and Mrs. Black, at a mutually agreed upon rate of interest of 12 percent. The selling broker has been able to find a local dentist who invests in second mortgages that are collateralized by local single-family houses that interest him. After checking out both the property and the references of the buyers, the dentist offers to buy the second mortgage from the sellers, Mr. and Mrs. White, at a discount of 15 percent off the face amount of $6,000. (A $6,000 note bought at a 15 percent discount equals $6,000 less $900 or $5,100. The dentist's $5,100 cash purchase of a $6,000 note paying 12 percent therefore bumps up its annual percentage return to the dentist to 14.1 percent. In other words, he will be receiving 12 percent interest on $6,000, or $720; however, he paid only $5,100, and $720 is 14.1 percent of $5,100.)

In this case, creative financing helped everybody all around. Thanks to the broker's creativeness, he's been able to complete the sale of the White's home at a full $60,000 price, which was most satisfactory to them. Although the Johnsons had opted to sell their second mortgage at a 15 percent discount for cash, they could have just as well elected to hold the second mortgage for the entire four years and earn the 12 percent interest, or to take the second mortgage they were holding and use it as collateral to get a loan if they were in need of money.

The purchase money mortgage concept allowed the cash-shy Blacks to complete the purchase of the White's home, which would have been beyond their financial reach without the use of this financing tool. The broker benefited, too. His knowledge of purchase money mortgages and the role they play in completing a sale meant that he was able to earn an important commission for himself. Finally, the dentist, as a third-party investor, was able to make a worthwhile investment that would give him the benefits of both safety and yield.

This is what is known as a win–win situation where everyone is able to achieve something of value.

SOME TIPS FOR GETTING THE BEST PURCHASE MONEY MORTGAGE

All aspects of a purchase money mortgage can be negotiated between the buyer and the seller. The different elements of this kind of second mortgage are:

1. The dollar amount of the second mortgage.

2. The rate of interest on the mortgage.

3. The term before the amount of the second mortgage loan must be paid back.

4. The mode of repayment of the second mortgage loan (whether it is to be paid back monthly, quarterly, semiannually, or annually).

5. Whether it is:

(a) A fully amortizing mortgage, meaning that re-payment schedule will include both interest and principal.

(b) A standing mortgage, meaning that interest-only payments will be made and then, at the end of the term, the entire principal amount will be paid off in one lump sum (called a balloon payment).

(c) A partially amortizing loan with a balloon payment due at the end of the term of the loan. For example: a $4,000 second mortgage loan for five years with interest-only payments for the first two years, then 5 percent amortization [5 percent of $4,000 equals $200 principal repayment] for years 3 and 4, and then the remaining balance to be paid off in the fifty year.)

Keep in mind that a purchase money mortgage be-tween a seller and a buyer is open for discussion in *all these condition areas*. Therefore, you can shoot for the best combination that you and your seller will find acceptable. In all likelihood, as the cash-shy buyer, you'll want: the largest amount of a second mortgage you can get, at the lowest rate of interest, with the longest pay-back period; a standing mortgage rather than an amortizing mortgage, with the most convenient mode of repayment.

I'm sure it will come as no great shock to you that the seller, in turn, will probably want the opposite for himself. The trick for the buyer is to establish what the most important conditions are for you to achieve in a purchase money mortgage arrangement with the seller and to establish what the conditions are that you are most willing to make concessions on. Initially you should press for the best conditions in all five areas above mentioned, knowing that you'll be willing to concede some point or two in exchange for your getting the points that are *really* important to you. In all cases, the seller should be made to feel that he pulled these concessions from you, so that he feels that he has "won" them. If he is left with this feeling he will probably be more prone to give you what you really wanted. For example, if getting (a) a large amount of a purchase money mortgage from the seller coupled with (b) a long payback period are vital to you, then be ready and willing possibly to make concessions on the other two or three areas of possibly a higher rate of interest for the seller and/or an amortizing rather than a standing repayment schedule. Look at it this way: If you have to give the seller another couple of percentage points of interest on his purchase money mortgage, how significant will it be to you in the long run if it helps you nail down the purchase of the house? If you had to go to a 16 percent interest rate on a $4,000 purchase money mortgage rather than a 14 percent rate, would the 2 percent difference which amounts to $80 per year be really important if it helped you get what you needed on other purchase money mortgage conditions? Bear in mind, too, that a higher yielding rate of interest will make the purchase money mortgage that much more attractive to a possible investor (such as the dentist in the previous example), a point that the seller or his broker will probably be mindful of.

There are other hidden benefits for the buyer, too, in the purchase money mortgage. Interest payments are tax-deductible, for one. This plus factor may soften to some degree the net effect of what you'll have to pay out in interest on the purchase money mortgage. Also, if a standing (interest-only) mortgage rather than an amortizing (repaying) mortgage is used, it means less cash being paid back periodically to the seller and more cash available to you. With inflation bound to be around for years to come, a large balloon payment at the end of the term of the second mortgage means you'd be paying back with cheaper dollars than if you were compelled to repay (amortize) the principal amount of the mortgage during its full term. You may have a fight on your hands in order to get the seller to concede to this point, but maybe you will have already conceded to him a higher rate of interest on the purchase money mortgage, or perhaps you will have conceded to pay the seller monthly interest points rather than quarterly or semiannual.

This business of striking a mutually acceptable set of purchase money conditions will require a lot of give and take. Therefore, the more you know about the techniques of negotiations, the better prepared you'll be to strike a deal that will be in your own best interests. Knowing about negotiation techniques (covered in detail in Chapter Six) is vitally important and can save you thousands of dollars in out-of-pocket money.

HOW TO SAVE THOUSANDS WITH DISCOUNTED BUY-BACKS

During the time you're negotiating with the seller, emotions can run pretty high. You are, after all, trying to buy the property as cheaply as possible and he is trying to get the highest possible price. If you can get the seller to extend you a purchase money mortgage with conditions you'll be comfortable with, then it might prove to your long-run interests to concede partially in negotiations on the price of his home. A seller may not be interested in making extensive concessions with the price of his home *at the time you're negotiating,* but if you've got a purchase money mortgage with him for four years, then two years or so after you've taken ownership, contact the previous owner. Suggest to him that you'd like to buy back the purchase money mortgage at a discount. It could be that you contacted him just at a time when the idea of getting cash for the mortgage he's holding would be most welcome and he'd be willing to take less cash on the remaining balance.

How much of a discount should you expect to get by paying off the mortgage early? That depends on how great the seller's need for cash is and on how much available cash you can round up (or borrow) to pay off the purchase money mortgage. It might be a 10 or 15, or as high as a 30 percent or more, discount. For instance, if the seller was holding your four-year $6,000 standing mortgage and you contacted him a year and a half after you owned the property, you might be reaching him just at a time when getting $4,500 in cash might be what he needs. From your point of view, that would represent a 25 percent discount. ($6,000 mortgage times 25 percent equals $1,500; $6,000 minus $1,500 equals $4,500.) In this particular example, you as the new current owner now, in a sense, actually own the property for $1,500 less than the price at the time of the closing when title passed to you. The interesting thing to remember is that *at the time when you were negotiating* the purchase of the house when emotions were running high, it's highly unlikely that your home seller would have chopped off $1,500 more on his price to satisfy you. What makes it different a year and a half or so after the actual transfer of title is that the emotions that ran high at the time of purchase have cooled, and the seller, in all likelihood will have dipped into some of the cash profits he derived from the sale and might be receptive to any kind of offer you come up with.

You can see now that the longer the term of the purchase money mortgage the better your chances of working out a discounted payoff later on. If, after all, the previous owner has a short term (a one-year, or possibly a two-year) purchase money mortgage with you, he might be less interested in this discount pay off arrangement than if the term of the purchase money mortgage was for three or four or five years and he had to wait for his money. In any case, always try to see if your purchase money mortgage holder will go for a discounted payoff of the mortgage and, once it's agreed on, have a lawyer put it in writing. The savings could run into the thousands.

HOW TO USE THE SELLER'S CREDIT TO HELP YOU BUY HIS PROPERTY

If you've made all kinds of attempts to get the seller to take back a second mortgage and he won't play, don't despair. There is another way to work with the seller that will benefit both himself and you.

If, as a cash-shy home buyer, you are borrowing some of the down payment money from a bank, you get a more favorable loan if you can get the home seller to co-sign your loan. All else being equal, this might improve both the interest rate on your loan and your pay-back arrangements at the bank. In addition, collateral, such as stocks, bonds, and saving certificates, almost always decrease the cost of borrowing money. Thus, if you contemplate borrowing bank funds, ask to borrow some collateral from the home seller in order to facilitate the sale of his house. Human nature being what it is, most potential lenders—even home owners—would be more agreeable to loaning out any stocks or bonds than to loaning their cash. Over the short term that you would need borrowed collateral, in order to make the deal more interesting to the seller you could offer to pay him an interest loan fee for the borrowed collateral (one or two percentage points might do it). Remember, the one or two percentage points you'd be paying him would be on top of the interest (if they're bonds) or dividends (if they're dividend-paying stocks) that the owner would continue to be receiving, so your offer would actually increase his total yield on his stock or bond.

To put the home owner's mind at ease, you could take out a short-term insurance policy to cover the period that you'd be borrowing his assets to use as collateral. If you do use any of these kinds of borrowing arrangements, you'd be well advised to have an attorney draw up appropriate papers that would circumvent any potential problem areas.

The whole thrust of this chapter has been to show the cash-shy home buyer that the home seller himself, particularly in today's unusual housing market, is a wonderful financing source that can be of tremendous help to put the deal together. More and more home buyers, out of necessity, are using these financing techniques with increasing success and, as a result, are now buying homes that otherwise would be out of their financial reach.

RED FLAG: Unless you are 100% assured of your source of future funds, do not get involved with a purchase money mortgage that will require your paying it off in one or two years in a balloon payment. You'd be surprised how quickly twelve to twenty-four months roll around and if you don't have the funds to make your final balloon payment, you'll have a problem on your hands. With your need-to-sell seller, however, your chances of getting a longer term in your purchase money mortgage (try to push for upward of five years) can be quite good. Negotiate to get as long as possible a term in order that you don't have the clock on yourself and so that the property can increase enough in value for you, if you so desire, to refinance in order to get money out of the property to meet your purchase money mortgage balloon payment that would be due.

CHAPTER FOUR

HOW TO
TALK TO A BANKER

In all likelihood, the biggest dollar "investor" in your home purchase will be the first mortgagee, the bank or thrift institution (that is, savings and loan association) that extends you the first mortgage money fundamental to the completion of your home purchase. It behooves you to know as much as possible about mortgaging banks and how you can get the best deal possible for yourself. Because the field of home mortgages has gone through explosive changes in the last few years, Chapter 7 will deal almost exclusively with the growing variety of mortgages that are being offered to today's borrower by institutional lenders.

Contrary to a misconception held by many people who do not deal with banks, all banks are *not* the same. Knowing something about the different kinds of banks beforehand will save you valuable time.

TYPES OF BANKS

The two major types of banks are savings banks and commercial banks. Savings banks, although they offer a wide range of other consumer services, concentrate a major part of their business on home mortgages as they have for years past. The public has rightfully associated savings banks with long-term (25 to 30 years), moderate fixed-interest rate home mortgages. Although fixed-interest rate mortgages are still available, the growing trend on the part of savings banks is toward the use of the variable-rate mortgage, wherein the rate of the mortgage can, at the election of the bank, be adjusted periodically. Depending on the type of variable-rate mortgage program, the rate could be up for review and adjusted once a year or once every two or three years. Thus, although savings banks are an important source for home mortgages, many of them no longer offer a fixed-rate mortgage program that renders the degree of financial security that comes with a fixed-interest rate mortgage.

The need for banks to have variable-rate mortgages in these days of rapidly changing money rates is clear enough. Banks need to be able to change their income (the interest they charge on the mortgages they have outstanding) as their expenses (the cost of the money they in turn must acquire) go through changes.

Unfortunately, the home owner who uses a variable-rate mortgage is now saddled with some of the financial risk that previously was resident with the bank. However, in order for savings banks to remain healthy and be in a position to offer home mortgages, it would appear that money-market conditions have virtually forced banks into offering mortgages of variable-rate kind.

COMMERCIAL BANKS

Commercial banks have had their main loan portfolio out with shorter-term loans (usually for a year or two) and catered to local business and consumer needs. However, commercial banks also offer home mortgages but the amount and their conditions vary from community to community. Commercial banks offering home mortgages are also offering variable-rate mortgages with a potential interest rate adjustment every few years, depending on the mortgage program. This approach is consistent with the way commercial banks have usually functioned. They loaned out their money for shorter intervals than savings banks and adjusted the rates more rapidly. Nowadays, savings banks, with their changeable interest rates every year or so, are beginning to take on the appearance of commercial banks in this regard.

CREDIT UNIONS

If you can join a credit union where you work or elsewhere, it might be in your best interest to do so, because credit unions have federal approval to make long-term mortgages and their rates have usually been competitive with those of other potential long-term mortgage resources.

THRIFT INSTITUTIONS

Thrift institutions, also referred to as savings and loan associations, are technically not banks but they offer many of the same customer services such as mortgages, home improvement loans, savings programs, and the like. Savings and loan associations are chartered either by the state or the federal government; hence you'll see names like "First Federal Savings & Loan Association." They are subject to state or federal regulations in their dealings in much the same way that commercial and savings banks are subject to regulations imposed by the Banking Commission. S & L's for years have been a major source of single-family home mortgages, and if these institutions can improve their deteriorating profit picture in the 80's, they can continue to be an important source of single-family home mortgages. Inasmuch as customers prefer to transfer their funds into higher-yielding money instruments, current money conditions mean, as far as the potential home buyer is concerned, that home mortgage money will be less available, more costly, and more involved with adverse financial conditions, such as penalties, points, and so on, now attached to mortgage loans.

DEALING WITH BANKS

All lending institutions have different reputations and lending sources. In a given community, certain banks will have liberal loan programs and others more conservative programs. Variations from bank to bank in lending and banking philosophy might come as a surprise to some who have little or no previous dealings with banks.

Although it is true that banks and thrift institutions work within the framework of state, federal or Banking Commission guidelines, there are gray areas in which each bank has, over a period of time, carved out for itself either a more liberal or a more conservative approach toward making loans. Obviously you'll stand a better chance of getting a favorable mortgage arrangement with the lending sources that have a more liberal reputation than with those that take a tighter approach to their loan portfolio. How do you find out about the reputations of lending sources in a community? Talk to people in the community, local businessmen, storekeepers, lawyers, and real estate brokers. All of these sources, particularly local real estate brokers and realtors, will give you valuable insight into the reputation of different local banks and S & L's. Two or three such contacts will not give you any real depth of information, so talk to as many individuals as you can.

For example, if you were trying to learn about local lending institutions with which you were not familiar and decided to touch base with only two or three, it could well be that the fourth could have told you that a certain bank places a lot of emphasis on how long you've been employed by your current employer. You could then slant your mortgage application with this factor in mind. In other words, little bits of information that you'll pick up could be valuable. The same rule applies to real estate brokers—five to ten is better than two or three. Keep in mind also that different real estate brokers have different kinds of relationships built up over the years with different lending sources, so therefore each conversation you have with them is bound to shed more light on this entire area for you.

All this research can be time-consuming. That is why this aspect of home buying can involve six months or more of your time. However, you need this time to educate yourself in all these different kinds of financial areas.

When gathering information, you'll find it helpful to mention nonconfidential information you've picked up from one source and see if it's confirmed, rejected, or modified by another. For example, one real estate broker could indicate that he's always had his best luck getting mortgages approved when he brings them to a certain loan officer at the bank. You might mention this to another real estate broker (without mentioning your source). The second broker might then give you additional information that confirms what you learned earlier. Thus, one bit of information stimulates a response and possibly additional information, and when all of it is put together, it helps build a picture about a bank or its loan philosophy. Knowing how to deal with a bank is important to your goal, so it's important not to overlook any clues you might pick up that you can put to use in making a loan application. And in the same way I suggested you learn about different local lending sources and their reputations, I also suggest you learn as much as you can about a given loan officer *before* you have extensive dealings with him.

SUMMARY

1. At any bank meeting, make sure you're neatly dressed and you conduct yourself in a businesslike manner by answering in a direct, forthright manner all questions put to you. As fundamental as that might sound, nonetheless many loan applicants come into a bank dressed in sloppy clothes, slouch in their seats, and generally do not emit an aura of confidence. The way you handle yourself and your general appearance

will either help or hinder to give the bank a feeling of confidence about your ability to meet possible mortgage payments.

2. When the loan officer or, more accurately, the mortgage committee, is determining what kind of terms to extend, they will review your credit record, family income, length and general stability of your employment, amount of debt you're handling, appraised value and all the characteristics of the house you want to purchase, and your future earning potential. Any additional information you can furnish with regard to promotions, raises, automatic salary increases, and so forth ought to be pointed out in your application.

3. Prior to making a mortgage application, if you have any major debt that you'll be obligated to pay in the next year or more, try to pay it off or at least make some sizeable reduction in the debt. It will strengthen your financial profile considerably.

4. If you have an account in the bank in which you're applying for a loan, don't be hesitant to push, plead, and prevail on your bank. Impress on them that you've been a loyal customer, that you've kept money at their bank notwithstanding that you could have gotten a higher yield in other instruments, and that you'd appreciate it if that loyalty could be reciprocated in a favorable mortgage application.

5. If the bank prides itself on being a local community bank, stressing that fact in its advertising, don't be hesitant to remind it of this when you go for a mortgage.

6. If the seller of the property has a good relationship with the bank, ask him to put in a good word for you. If he's a real heavyweight at the bank, the bank would

give some second thoughts to your mortgage application as they might not want to jeopardize their relationship with a good account.

7. Your employer or the seller's employer, if they have accounts at the bank where you're looking to get your mortgage, can be invaluable to you at a time like this. A business would have a fairly substantial banking account, and a few well-placed telephone calls from a corporate officer who wanted to help a valued employee might work wonders.

8. Lawyers, too, can help to put in a good word for you, as can established real estate brokers who have cultivated relationships with local lenders. Sometimes real estate brokers can be prevailed upon to leave part of their commission earnings from the transaction with the mortgaging bank if the bank will then consider the mortgage application favorable. I've seen established real estate brokers, during the tightest money periods, go to a bank where they've had a long and mutually beneficial banking relationship and push to get mortgage loans through after talking with the bank president, whereas other brokers couldn't get to first base.

9. Clout: If you don't have it, borrow it! Even if your uncle has not been your favorite person, if you can get him to transfer some big bucks to the mortgaging bank you want to work with, give it a shot.

MORTGAGE SHOPPING

Most professional real estate brokerage firms will be able to provide you with a chart of what local banks are offering in terms of mortgage funds, rates, and conditions. Because of the volatility of money these days, on-the-ball firms will update this chart almost weekly so they have the latest local information that relates to mortgage interest rates, percentage of cash-down requirements, terms of loan, types of loan, prepayment penalty conditions, points to be paid, and so on. From this chart you will be able to evaluate, with your broker's help, which lending source offers you the most favorable terms and conditions. Together, you and your broker will examine the bank's requirements in light of how much available cash-down funds you have, how much debt service you feel you can handle, how many points (one point being equivalent to one percentage point of the amount of the mortgage) you can live with, and other considerations, such as bank origination fees or prepayment penalties (a prepayment penalty is a percentage figure, stipulated in the mortgage documents, that you are required to pay the bank if you pay off the mortgage before its full term expires).

You'll want to weigh all these factors in light of your ready cash available for the down payment, your need to have additional dollars for closing fees and a general reserve contingency, and your ability to handle the monthly mortgage and other related cost factors (insurance, taxes, and the like). Therefore, you'll want to elect the mortgage program offered by the lending institution that gives you the best opportunity to apply a certain degree of leverage. Leverage is the concept of being able to buy and control a large asset (such as a house) with the least amount of your own out-of-pocket cash. In this light, you will want to review the different mortgage conditions offered by the various lending sources to see which source requires the least expensive combination of smallest cash-down payment (including points) in conjunction with the least costly debt service (that is, monthly mortgage payments).

Your monthly mortgage payments will be made up of return of principal to the lender (called amortization) plus interest paid on the principal balance. The two elements that will affect how much this monthly debt service cost will be are the interest rate on the mortgage and the length (term) of the mortgage. On a fixed-rate mortgage, the longer the term of the pay-back period, the less your monthly mortgage payment will be. As an example, a $50,000 mortgage at 15 percent over a 20-year term would require monthly payments of $658.40; a 30-year term would require $632.22 a month in payments. However it must be pointed out that paying back a mortgage loan over a longer period of time will cost more in total interest payments, but there are other considerations that take on importance in this regard.

The greater total interest payments made on a longer-term mortgage come into full effect only if you hold the mortgage for its full term. In all likelihood, you'll have sold your home long before that time. The national average on the length of mortgage-holding is seven years. Also, the interest on mortgage payments is a tax-deductible item; therefore, the larger the interest payments made, the more tax-deductible dollars available to lower your federal taxable income.

Buying with selective leverage is something real estate investors aim toward because it conserves their cash and their financial exposure, keeps additional cash available for other investments or as a reserve for unforeseen contingencies, and increases the potential percentage return as their investment increases in market value. The same is true for private home financing. In a sense, leverage techniques permit you to *buy now* with less of your cash and more of other people's money. In fact, most creative financing techniques dealing with the use of other people's money and the techniques for the payment of out-of-pocket cash are based on the premise that you'll be able to meet future financial commitments with future income or other anticipated sources of dollars, and from the increased value of your home. There is nothing immoral or illegal in this approach: For real estate investors, it is standard, legitimate business practice.

Shopping for a mortgage, contrary to popular opinion, does not mean getting a quote from one, two, or three local lending sources, but requires an extensive, systematic search for the best possible deal.

Prepare a chart, and on the left side indicate all the items that you'd want to know concerning a possible mortgage being offered to you, such as interest rate, whether the rate is fixed or variable, the term of the mortgage, percentage of cash down required, the number of points required, any prepayment penalty conditions, and so on. Then visit as many banks or savings and loan associations as you can that might service your mortgage needs. Savings and loan associations by law can extend mortgages up to a 100-mile radius. This vastly expands your possible sources. Do not just talk to one, two, or three possible lending sources and from that assume that all lending sources will have the same story to tell you. In order to get the best possible overall mortgage for yourself, you should contact, in person where possible, from five to ten lending sources. Why so many? Because different lending sources have different, changing needs at different times and there is no way that you can anticipate what kind of mortgage package and costs will be offered unless you make *direct contact*. What a lender was prepared to offer to do, mortgage-wise, 30 to 60 to 90 days ago, is different than what they're prepared to offer you today. Also, what a possible mortgage lender was willing to offer a friend, associate or acquaintance of yours has little or nothing to do with what they might, or might not, be willing to offer you. Also, different lenders might perceive you differently as to security, risk and growth, and other areas of influence you might be able to bring to bear.

This brings to mind an acquaintance of mine, a seller of mutual fund plans, who was on the verge of buying his first home. We discussed this concept of mortgage shopping and as a result of our initial meeting he made a chart such as the one I have described. He then went out and got mortgage cost quotations from ten different lending sources, and thanks to his extensive mortgage research efforts he not only was made aware of the wide range in mortgage costs but was able to select the one program that best fit his personal financial needs. My friend figured that the lending source mortgage program he finally decided on, and from whom he subsequently got his mortgage, saved him thousands of dollars over the life of the mortgage. As a consequence, the time he spent in research was well worth the extra effort he used visiting different banks and S & L's, learning what their mortgage programs were.

SHOPPING FOR
MOTIVATED SELLERS

Basic to your ability to get the best home-buying deal with the least amount of out-of-pocket cash will be your ability to deal with motivated sellers. The two basic broad categories of home sellers are:

1. Nonpressured home sellers selling primarily for profit.

2. Need-to-sell situations wherein the home owner/seller is under some degree of pressure.

I want to encourage you, in order for you to satisfy your low-cash home-ownership goals, to search out need-to-sell situations. They will be the ones that will be the most responsive to your negotiation tactics and your creative financing techniques. It stands to reason that if a home seller is under no pressure whatsoever, it's going to be a lot tougher to get the kind of deal you seek.

Need-to-sell situations usually grow out of any of the following circumstances:

1. A marriage and/or a business split-up.

2. Deteriorating physical health and the desire to get out from under home-ownership responsibilities.

3. Retirement to a warmer climate.

4. Job opportunities in another community.

5. Strong interest in or even prior commitment to another home.

6. Imperative requirement for home repairs (because of neglect, fire, and so on) that the owner is not interested in completing.

7. Estate sales or pending foreclosure sales.

These are the kinds of sellers that will lead you to an affordable financing framework for yourself. How do you find need-to-sell situations? Tell each real estate broker or realtor you contact that you're looking for need-to-sell situations (and enumerate some of these general categories mentioned). It is when you and your real estate broker understand the needs of sellers that you'll be able to come up with an offer or a form of financing that will *fit the seller's needs*, as well as your own goals.

Any experienced real estate broker can give you dozens of examples of situations in which alert potential buyers, sensitive to the needs of need-to-sell sellers, were able to buy favorably because they discovered the cause of the seller's need to sell and then structured their offers to fill these needs. It's another way of saying, find out where it hurts and then relieve the cause of the pain if you want to strike a deal.

This country's supply of need-to-sell situations will be increasing as the financial uncertainties of our time remain. The expansion of consumer credit coupled with inflation and unemployment has put many people under financial pressures where many will be forced into becoming home sellers. This kind of unsettled financial climate has even permeated many marriages and businesses, thereby giving rise to additional pressured home sellers. Then, too, with a growing older population in America, the desire to move to Sun Belt states has transformed other home owners into motivated sellers.

In essence, the market for the cash-shy potential home buyer will be richest in need-to-sell situations.

CHAPTER FIVE

HOW TO HANDLE A BROKER

Anytime you enter dealings with another individual who has more experience in a certain area than you do, you become vulnerable. The other party will stand a better chance of achieving his personal needs, which might not be consistent with your own. So you do not have to merely hope the other party's needs are consistent with yours. I want to help move you out of amateur status quickly and achieve parity with the individuals with whom you must deal in real estate transactions. Unless you have a strong sales or business background, you will be dealing with real estate salespeople whose day-in, day-out experience and expertise in sales exceed your own. Professional real estate salespeople who have extensive selling experience not only will have learned *how* to present a property in its most favorable light but will also have learned how to overcome buyer objections. Experienced salespeople know how to find out what a prospective buyer's needs are and present their product in such a way that the property will fulfill those needs. This approach is basic to all successful sales transactions. This chapter will give you some insight into how real estate salespeople handle themselves and you as the buyer, and will prepare you for the seller–buyer encounter.

All commissioned sales agents are basically in business for themselves. If you start out with this understanding that real estate salespeople make their living not by just *presenting* houses but by *selling* houses, you will become a more realistic buyer. Armed with this seemingly small insight, you can begin to approach your home-searching activity with a more jaundiced eye. Even the most professional real estate broker does not have to be your complete confidant in all aspects of your house hunting or negotiating. Be selective in what you say because what you bring out will be viewed in light of how it can be used to help *sell you* a given house. If, for example, you have a rock-bottom price or a fixed cash amount that you know you can afford to spend, that bottom figure should remain with you *alone*. Remember, the broker is *not* your partner. He is an independent third party that in all likelihood is trying to get the seller to reduce his price or conditions of sale while at the same time getting you to increase your offer or cash. In fact, by contract, he represents the seller!

HINTS: Work with real estate brokers who are experienced in a specific geographic area that interests you. Such a broker will, in all likelihood, have important exclusive listings and would be in a favorable position to hear about need-to-sell situations as they come on the market—in many cases *before* they come on the market. Successful brokerage firms get their listings in many cases from referrals because they have been active for a number of years. Therefore, when you're dealing with a well-established firm, try to work with an experienced broker rather than someone new to real estate or new to the community. You shouldn't have to contend with anyone who doesn't have a depth of experience in both the area you're interested in and the type of house situation you're looking for.

If you don't know who to contact in a given real estate firm, you might try a technique of mine. Simply ask for the most successful real estate broker or salesperson in the organization. There might be a few self-conscious chuckles in the office background but, rest assured, usually one or two names are offered. As in most businesses, 80 percent of the sales usually come from 20 percent of the sales force, and most people in real estate offices know who among their peers make up that 20 percent. Successful real estate salesmen are going to be able to help you get what you want. *The unsuccessful real estate people do not have either the experience, the know-how, or the drive, persistence, and negotiating skills to help.* This is an important point to keep in mind; otherwise you'll find yourself wasting valuable time being chauffeured around to houses that are inappropriate and accompanied by an inexperienced broker who can't help you in the all-important financing and negotiating aspects of your purchase.

A brokerage firm located thirty or forty miles from where you want to buy probably will not be much help. They won't be well-known in the community and cannot secure the good listings or even know about need-to-sell situations as they come onto the market. Moreover, experienced local real estate brokers with good exclusive listings do not always feel they have to co-broker their valuable listings with another. If a listing is good, the local firm will feel they can sell it without having to split their commissions.

In line with this, knowing what motivates the broker will give you more insight too. The more you know about his motivations, the more you'll be able to read between the lines. If you were a selling agent and you felt you had two products both of which could fit a given customer's needs, but if one product yielded a full commission and the other only a partial commission, would you give them equal attention? Of course not. Then again, the truly professional real estate broker, who is both experienced and secure in his work, will want to satisfy the needs of the customers regardless of whether a listing is exclusive or co-brokered.

Because of your particular home-buying needs (that is, an affordable house emanating from a need-to-sell situation coupled with creative financing), you will be best served to work with as many brokers as you feel you can. By making your needs known to several, you can increase your chances of finding what you're looking for. A one-broker situation with the broker willing to spend exhaustive time with a buyer is more likely to arise where the prospect is strong financially and looking for an important piece of property. Take your clue, then, from the brokers. They know from experience that their best chance of consummating a sale comes from working with *many* prospective buyers. In the same light, you should work with as many experienced brokers as you can who have a depth of knowledge about the community that interests you as well as experience with creative financing and the fine art of negotiating.

It's also important to know the terminology used by brokers as it relates to a listed property. An Exclusive Right to Sell listing means that the broker will have the exclusive right to sell the property, subject to the rate of commission specified, the conditions therein, and the length of time specified in the listing agreement which is the contract for services between the seller and the broker. Under an Exclusive Right to Sell arrangement, the listing broker will be entitled to a commission whether he sells the property or the home owner sells it himself. This latter aspect of the Exclusive Right to Sell listing is structured in this way because the broker's cost of marketing the house (that is, advertising, showing the property, related expenses such as correspondence, telephone calls, and so on) would be incurred notwithstanding who finally sold the property. Furthermore, the broker's time dedicated to marketing the house is considered time taken away from marketing other saleable houses.

The second type of listing is called an Exclusive Listing. It provides that the owner has the right to sell the property himself without any obligation to pay a commission to the listing broker.

The third type of listing is the Open Listing, which, as the name implies, is a listing that is open to as many brokers as the home seller wishes. From the broker's point of view, this is the least desirable type of listing to carry.

It stands to reason that the experienced broker will want to get an Exclusive Right to Sell listing, which will give him the financial security to plan a full-scale marketing program to sell the property. On the other hand, the Exclusive Listing still gives the broker a goodly amount of financial security and is quite common. The third type, the Open Listing, gives him the least amount of financial security and therefore he has that much less incentive to promote, advertise, and market the property inasmuch as any other broker who has the listing could sell the house and get the commission.

If the broker (or his firm) is a member of a local Multiple Listing Service, then even though he has an Exclusive Listing, he may share his exclusive with his fellow multiple listing members. Under this arrangement, if he sells his exclusive himself he will get the full commission. However, if another member of the multiple listing service consummates the sale, then the commission is split and the listing broker gets the smaller share.

Armed with this insight into the three different kinds of listing arrangements that prevail in the real estate industry, you can now utilize it to benefit yourself.

The broker who has next to nothing in the way of a listings inventory of homes for sale is not going to be for you. This broker either is too new or has some other problem preventing his getting the all-important listings. Listings are the very lifeblood of a growing real estate office, for without an inventory of houses to sell they are not in business. Houses for sale are a broker's stock-in-trade.

Additionally, if the majority of a given broker's listings are overpriced, this represents a clear signal to you that you're dealing with the wrong real estate office. A vast amount of overpriced property listings could indicate either a lack of knowledge on the broker's part about current market values or, worse yet, a lack of honesty on his part as it relates to his clients—the sellers. Though they are fortunately in the minority, there are some brokers who, in their desire to get listings, will list a house well above current market price in order to satisfy the seller's unrealistic desire to make a killing with the sale of his home.

Another type of broker who is not going to be helpful to you is one who has mostly multiple listings, co-broker listings, and open listings. Generally, this kind of broker is missing the all-important exclusive listings which invariably go to the established, respected local firm that has a well-earned reputation from a long list of favorable sales. The seasoned broker with exclusive listings on realistically priced property will rely primarily on his own selling efforts. He doesn't have to share his commission with another firm and probably will look to the Multiple Listing Service to help him sell his less than hot properties, although it is not to be assumed that properties that are on MLS are a less attractive product.

Finally, the promoter, high-pressure salesman is also not going to be of any lasting help. He is interested only in pushing the buyer into something that fits his own needs, which does not mean it fits *the buyer's* needs. Fortunately, this type of broker is also in the minority and usually has a short-lived business career in a community. Word soon gets out that he's looking for the fast buck and the fast sale, and that eventually puts the kibosh on his career. In all likelihood, he wouldn't be getting the leads or listings on the need-to-sell situations. The generally negative reputation of this kind of broker would probably discourage a need-to-sell seller to list with him.

Real estate, like all areas of business, has its quota of people who do not put much stock in personal integrity. It will be your job to seek out those brokers who not only have needed valuable experience but possess integrity. You can size up a broker several ways. Be mindful of how he handles you. If he comes on as a fast-talking promoter or makes deceitful statements or indicates devious tactics, be careful. For example, although it's illegal, a less than honest broker could suggest that a contract of sale on a property be inflated in order that a bigger mortgage might be obtained thereby requiring less up front cash.

It is also wise to learn to listen to how and what brokers say to other brokers or prospects on the telephone while you're in their office. If you hear them making misleading statements or exaggerating claims, then let that be a red flag.

Generally if a broker doesn't take the time to ask you questions about *your* needs, you can be pretty well assured that he is inexperienced or untrained. In either case, the chances of his being of real help to you are minimal. Or, if his main thrust seems to be to persuade you to buy where he can make the biggest commission rather than fit *your* needs, then be on the alert!

Finally, there's the broker who is always advertising unbelievable buys that always seem to vanish when you get to his office. That has shades of the old "bait and switch" tactic, where the prospect is baited and then switched into "the better model for you." Or, as a friend of mine puts it, "If it sounds too good to be true, then chances are it probably is!"

Notwithstanding all the consumer-oriented legislation that's found its way into our society in the last decade, it's still best to approach the buying process with a heady dose of the *caveat emptor* concept. There are three parties to any real estate transaction: a buyer, a broker, and a seller. Of the three the buyer is the only one who's putting money on the table. That thought alone ought to be sobering enough for anyone.

Another approach when looking for property to buy is always to endeavor to find at least two or three properties of genuine interest to you. I have found from experience that having the option of being interested in more than one property at a time allows me to then become a tougher and a better buyer, pushing for better price, terms, and conditions, knowing that if I don't get the first property under terms and conditions I want, then I still have the others to pursue. Or, as someone wisely once said, "Properties are like buses. If I don't get this one I'll get the next one that comes along." If you keep this same approach in mind, you will be a better, more sophisticated buyer who will stand a better chance to buy the home you want at a better price and under more favorable conditions. Or, as a friend I know puts it, you should care, but not too much. By finding *more* than one house of interest, you will thereby tend not to over-determine its importance to you and, as a result, you'll make a better deal for yourself.

As a buyer, you have more power than you might realize. Why? Because without a buyer there's no deal, and "no deal" to a broker means no commission, so keep in mind the vital role of importance you play. Keep in mind, too, that real estate brokers make their living showing and selling property. In this light, there is no reason for you to feel guilty if a broker has shown you many different houses, none of which fits your needs. Inexperienced first-time buyers sometimes feel, out of a sense of guilt, that they're under some type of obligation to buy from the broker who's shown the most houses. No such law is on the books, so avoid the feeling; it can cost you money you don't want to spend on something you don't really want.

There are other ways to sense when you're dealing with an experienced broker. The experienced salesperson will not fight you when you bring up an objection about the property. They are too smart to respond with a "you're wrong on that point" kind of answer. Chances are, if you do bring up an objection, experienced salespeople will not choose to respond. They know many buyers feel the need to make *some* kind of comment in order not to appear stupid or a pushover, and they realize if the objection is valid it will be raised again later.

In answering an objection, the experienced real estate

salesperson will minimize the effect of the buyer's objection by some phrase such as "That's an interesting point," or "I know what you mean, but . . ." or, "I agree with your thinking; however don't lose sight of . . .," or "You may have a point there; however. . . ." In this situation, the salesman isn't agreeing with you but he's acknowledging your objection and conveying the impression that he's taken it under consideration; instead of fighting you on the question he wants you to feel he is giving you new information that more than compensates for your objection.

These are all good selling tactics and I want you to recognize them as such so that you can evaluate them accordingly. They will guide you to the fact that you're dealing with a successful and experienced broker or salesperson. Selling is the name of the game and everything else is secondary. Why is this fact important to you? *Because a strong real estate broker who really knows how to sell will be vital to you: he can "sell" your offer to the home owner.* Let's face it: You're probably going to be making a low-cash, highly leveraged offer on a property at a price below its offered market price, and one of the best things you'll want going for you is a topflight salesman (or saleswoman) who will know how to overcome and/or moderate the objections of the seller to your offers! Good sellers are good negotiators and an experienced broker who's a good salesman and negotiator can literally make or break the entire deal for you!

When you've made contact with several brokers who you feel have both the experience and sales know-how to be of help to you, you should endeavor to ingratiate yourself with them and stimulate their best efforts on your behalf. Be respectful of their time, which is one of their most valuable commodities next to their listing inventory. If you can't keep an appointment, notify them far enough in advance so it can be rescheduled. If I had a nickel for every broker who's sat around waiting for a prospect that never showed up for an appointment or called to cancel it, I could retire a very wealthy man! Even if it looks like you'll be late for an appointment, at least call and alert the broker accordingly. This show of good manners and consideration on your part will distinguish you as one of the genuinely nice people in this world. Be forthright and tell your broker what your needs are in terms of property, price, neighborhood, available cash, your interest in need-to-sell situations and in properties purchasable under creative financing techniques. The more an experienced broker knows about your needs and limitations, the quicker, better, more effective help he can be to you.

Finally, let the broker know that you can possibly refer him to other buyers or sellers who might have need of his services. Contacts that you might have among your friends, business contacts, and church or fraternal organizations will heighten his interest in doing an outstanding job for you.

In the final analysis, a good broker will save you both time and money in a host of ways. He will make an effort to discover your specific needs and may have the listings that will fit these needs. He will know about local financing sources and creative financing techniques, and will be able effectively to negotiate your needs to the seller. He can help smooth the way in your dealings with appraisers, bankers, lawyers, town officials, and other parties to any final sales agreement.

CHAPTER SIX

HOW TO USE EFFECTIVE NEGOTIATING TECHNIQUES

Effective negotiating is the most important element at your disposal to help you buy an affordable house. Negotiation skills can replace money, but money can never take the place of a good negotiator. After all, you could have a good knowledge of how to work with brokers, what the different creative financing techniques are, and how banks work with different types of mortgages, but if you don't know how to negotiate effectively for these things, then all your knowledge will be of little real value. If you and your broker don't know the insider techniques of bargaining to get what you want, then *all* the other knowledge you may have absorbed is only of limited value.

Negotiating, or bargaining, is a way of life in certain parts of the world. The game of give and take between buyer and seller is, in these other countries, almost a national pastime, to the point that it would be unthinkable for a buyer to pay full price for an article and deprive the seller of the pleasure of haggling to get the buyer to increase his price. Fortunately, in this country most goods and services are sold at full price. The major exceptions are automobiles and houses. Thus it is a forgone conclusion that when it comes to a real estate transaction, negotiation will take place.

Negotiation is inevitable primarily because there is no such thing as a *fixed* price on a property in the same way as there is on a can of beans at the local supermarket. On the contrary, real estate prices are arrived at through the process of negotiation that derives its movement from the needs and motivations of buyer and seller. In fact, when one considers that the needs of the average seller to get the highest possible price are diametrically opposed to the needs of the average buyer to buy at the least cost, it's a wonder that real estate transactions ever come to a mutually acceptable conclusion at all!

The single most important factor that will make the most impact on the negotiation process resides in one word: motivation. People's emotional needs, which are at the basis of their motivation, will invariably play a larger role in the negotiation process than will the property itself. What this means to you as a cash-shy buyer looking for an affordable house in a market where prices are too high and the cost of mortgage money skyrockets is that *only through your knowledge of the needs of the seller, coupled with your ability to couch your offer in terms that will attempt to fulfill those needs, will you be able to get what you want*. If you can fulfill, or come close to filling, the needs of the other party, they in turn will then fulfill, or come close to filling your needs as a buyer. In some real estate circles this is referred to as win–win negotiation, where both parties come away feeling they have made a satisfactory arrangement.

This requires buyers to view things in terms of the

other person's needs. *If you want to sell a home owner on selling his house to you on your terms, then you'll have to fulfill* his *needs.* You will have to fulfill his needs *first* because, as the buyer, you're the one that's taking the initiative—you're the one that's courting the buyer—you are the suitor because they (the sellers) have something you want (that is, their house at a price and conditions you can live with). Taking your mind off your own needs, separating limiting factors in your own ego or financial requirements, and concentrating a good amount of your time, energy, and investigative talents in finding out about your seller are the keys to getting the property you desire. If the negotiation process is similar to a battle, then it behooves you to do what every good general does: Learn everything you can about your "enemy"—their strengths, weaknesses, needs, hopes. Scout out the "enemy" to know what you'll be contending with, which, frankly, is just what the big-league football and/or baseball teams do when they scout out the opposition in order that they can be better prepared for their future dealings with their opposition.

There are several avenues available to you that will give you insight into the needs of the seller. Of course there is the real estate agent, who should have probed enough to understand the reasons why the seller wants to sell. You'll want to know if the seller wants a quick or delayed sale, and why; how long the property has been on the market; if there were other offers made on the property, and when; if the seller is an experienced businessperson seasoned in negotiation or if he is a first-time seller; and how long the seller has owned the property and what the size of the equity in the property is.

Another valuable source of information about your seller can come from people in the community (local bankers, tradesmen, lawyers, and others) who might give you additional insight. Perhaps social, fraternal, or religious organizations might furnish additional information. For example, an investor friend was interested in making an offer on a small rental property that had been foreclosed and was now owned by the bank. My investor friend, who was a strong believer in the "know thy seller" concept, decided to snoop around and learn as much as he could about the bank. Good fortune was with him, for sitting at a bar next to him several weeks after he first viewed the property was someone indirectly involved with the bank who knew the history of its involvement with the foreclosed rental property. This individual told my friend that the bank was interested in disposing of the property because the state bank examiners were going to be coming around on their periodic visit, and one thing bank examiners don't like to see on the books of a bank is an REO (Real Estate Owned), bank talk for real estate that they own because they have had to foreclose on it. Armed with this valuable information, my friend knew what his tactic would be, and he was able to purchase the property with highly favored conditions of sale that gave him a leveraged, low-cash offer in exchange for a reasonable price and a quick sale, which is precisely what the bank needed.

It will be to your benefit to try to find out things such as: Is the seller experienced, is the seller abrupt in his dealings and quick to come to decisions, or is he the type that takes his time and is slow in making a decision and generally indecisive . . . ? Many times, these and/or other personality characteristics are known about a seller within the industry and/or business community where he works, and once you've gained this additional insight, you'll at least know what kind of general behavior you might expect and therefore can adopt your tactics accordingly (although, frankly, when it comes to selling and negotiating on the price of one's home that's for sale, emotions can run fever high and irrational acts, sometimes out of character, have been known to come into play).

Moreover, as a buyer, you have several areas of power for yourself that are to your advantage. Always keep in mind the fact that you are the one that calls the shots, that gets the entire "game into play" because nothing happens, nor can it happen, until you make an offer on a piece of property. Even when your initial offer is refused and the seller comes back with a counteroffer, it is still you who decides if you want to keep the ball in play with another offer. Frankly, I've been a buyer many times and a seller many times, and I can tell you without a moment's hesitation that you as the buyer are holding most of the good cards. What you, as the buyer, probably don't realize is that the seller has to wait for someone to come by who's interested enough to make an offer. The seller (and most sellers are usually, but not always, more anxious to sell than you are to buy) bedevils himself with a variety of worries: Will an interested buyer come on the scene? Will the buyer's initial offer be his last offer? How much more will the buyer increase his offer? Has the buyer found another property that interests him? Has the buyer lost interest considering the time lapse between offers? Indeed the seller is not unlike the fisherman who has to keep his baited line dangling in the water for what seems like an eternity in the patient hope that he'll eventually get a nibble.

There's a good reason why you, as the buyer, are more in the driver's seat than the seller actually is: First off, you, and you alone, know how much you're willing to pay for the property. After all, the seller does not know what's in your mind and can only at best guess as to how high he can get you to raise your price. Frankly, he's shooting in the dark when it comes to knowing what you'll pay for the property, whereas *you, as the buyer, will know in your mind just how far you'll be willing to go in upward price concessions, and no farther*. And remember, your top price you'll be willing to go to should be your own private business (and not your broker's who, after all, is not your partner).

However, the broker can play a valuable role *on your behalf* in the negotiation process because negotiating through him, rather than directly with a seller, avoids any possible emotional outbursts, or rash statements by either side. A seasoned real estate broker who's experienced in negotiation can make or break a transaction and that is to your advantage, too. He will know how to handle a seller in order to get the desired result. After all, he wants the sale much as the seller wants to sell and the buyer to buy.

NEGOTIATING PRICE

There are probably as many theories on offering price as there are pebbles on a beach. However, your initial offering price will invariably relate to just *how* pressured the seller is to sell and *how long* the property has been on the market. Any initial price offer *could* be 5 to 10 percent below the seller's asking price, all the way up to 15 to 25 percent off the seller's price, depending upon the overall condition of the property. However, before you make your initial offer, you should have a game plan as to how high you'll be willing to go.

You should have an initial price in mind, as well as a

target price range (a range within which you'd be most satisfied to buy), and a *top price range* (the highest price you can possibly handle). In all likelihood, the final price you pay will be somewhere between the top of your *target price range* and the lower end of your *top price range*. This might work out as follows: Property is offered at $60,000. Your *initial offer* is $51,000 (15 percent less than asked). Your *target price range* is $53,000 to $54,000, and your *top price range* is $55,000 to $56,000. After a series of offers and counteroffers, you purchased the property at $55,500!

SELLER NEEDS

Returning to the key words of *motivation* and *seller needs*, all seller's needs can be broken down to a number of general areas, and if you can couch your offers to appeal to the seller's needs, you'll help your cause immeasurably.

Pride. Most home owners have an important sense of pride about their home. Selling their home is a highly emotional and personal experience. Your sincere compliments about the seller's home not only will please them and make them feel that they'll be selling to someone who really appreciates the home, but might do much to smooth the negotiation process and put you in a favorable position.

Profit. The seller with this need will see his sale primarily in terms of the kind of profit he feels he must make in the transaction. This seller may be so concerned with price that all else in the transaction is secondary. Strange as it may sound, this is a weakness on the seller's part that you can capitalize on. Why?

Because seasoned real estate investors know from experience that conditions of sale are more important than the price of the property. Remember "I'll buy on my terms and your price, or my price and your terms"?

Here are some exaggerated illustrations of this concept of conditions of sale being more important than price. Say the seller wants $65,000 for his house, even though comparable sales indicate it should realistically sell for $55,000. You offer, without any negotiation, the full asking price subject to your conditions of sale, which are: $500 cash down and the balance at the rate of $100 per month until the balance is paid in full.

Obversely, you could seek to buy at your price and on the seller's terms as follows: You offer all the cash the seller wants down subject to your getting exactly what you want in price for property. Let's say, $15,000 cash down against a $15,000 offering price for the seller's $45,000 home!

Realistically, the seller is *not* going to get it *both* ways, which, of course, doesn't prevent him from trying to get his full price and best conditions any more than it prevents the buyer from trying to get *his* price and *his* terms. Of course, what this means is that *both price and conditions of sale are variable and can be negotiated to your advantage*.

When you've found out what the seller's needs are, you'll be able to present your offer in terms of his needs. For example, if a quick sale because of health, or relocation, or financial pressures is vitally important to the seller, then each time you make an offer or counteroffer, you can make each offer with less cash down but with ever-increasing closing dates.

In this kind of trade-off be careful not to give everything away on your first offer, but spread it out so that

110

each subsequent offer and counteroffer is more appealing than the last.

Often a seller's need for love and approval can be an area of opportunity for the buyer. For example, a seller's need to get what his neighbor got for his house when he sold it might give you insight into the seller's emotional needs. If you overhear comments such as these when viewing a home, consider carefully how you may utilize them when you're making your initial and subsequent offers.

Pressure. Most sellers in need-to-sell situations are generally nervous by virtue of the situation itself. Keep the seller's nervousness in *your* mind because it will give you power in the negotiating process. *The seller's need to sell is what puts you in an advantageous position in the negotiating process.*

The nervous seller, once you've expressed interest in the property and made an initial offer, is concerned that he will lose the sale. Therefore, your strategy should be to keep the negotiating process strung out for as long as you can. The longer you can keep the negotiating process going, the more time the seller has invested and the more edgy he becomes as to whether he's going to get his completed sale or not. With a bigger investment in time and the entire negotiating process stretched out over as many days and/or weeks as you can stretch it into, the more the seller, near the end of the negotiating process, is more likely to say to himself, "Oh, what the heck, I might as well make some of the concessions that this buyer wants *'cause I've spent so much time already on it* and, anyhow, who knows how long it will be before I get another buyer who seems as interested as this guy." It is true that you too will have invested the time, but it will have been done at your design in order to get the seller to come around to your way of thinking.

111

Time is one of the most potent forces you have as a negotiator, and you can use it as a strong force. Herb Cohen, author of *You Can Negotiate Anything,* points out in his book the example of the Japanese businessmen's dealings with an American businessman. Without the visiting American's knowledge, the Japanese found out when he had booked his return flight. Armed with this information, the Japanese spent the first week sightseeing with their American guest. When the American expressed interest in getting started with the business discussions, the Japanese put him off with more entertaining. The Japanese kept this up for weeks until only a few days before his intended departure, when the American was getting impatient to get started. Finally, two days before his departure, the Japanese decided to sit down to talk, knowing that the American had put the clock on himself. The result was the Japanese got more favorable terms.

The moral of this cautionary tale is simple: always try to *put the clock* on the *other person.* The process puts a high degree of pressure on the other side and leaves you in a stronger position. For example, you could make your offer subject to hearing from the seller by such and such a date because "you have to leave town on business by that date." You can create as many clock cut-off dates as your imagination can produce. The important thing is to put a sense of urgency into the other party's thinking and thereby place him at a disadvantage.

TACTICS

Your initial offer or subsequent counteroffers must convey the feeling that each offer is firm and final. To do otherwise would tip the other side off to the fact that you could be bluffing. However, if you decide to make an advancement beyond your previous offer, you can always say something like, "I've had more opportunity to review your proposal again, and I'm prepared to do such and such if you, in turn, can do such and such."

This brings up an important tactic for you to use in any series of offers and counteroffers. *Never make a concession of value to the other party unless you extract a concession of equal weight*. The use of this concept is vital to your success in negotiating; otherwise you'd be giving up something of value and getting nothing in return.

NEGOTIATING VARIABLES

The price of the house, the amount of cash down, the amount of cash to be paid at the closing, the amount that might be paid at a later date—"I'll tell you what, Mr. Seller, I'll pay the $15,000 cash down you insist on but I'll pay you $5,000 at the day of the closing, $5,000 six months later, and the final $5,000 six months from that date"—and the rate of interest are important variables up for negotiation. Other variables are the amount of a purchase money mortgage and the length of term of such a mortgage. In this regard, it is important to note that buying with a purchase money mortgage from the seller, it is best to try to get a five-year term or more. Anything less than that means that the property will have to *appreciate fast enough and the future financing costs be reasonable enough* for you to refinance the property comfortably enough to get sufficient money out of the property's increased equity in order to pay off your remaining balance on the purchase money mortgage and still handle the probable higher interest rates on the new, larger first mortgage. Maybe you could live with a three-year purchase money mortgage payoff but, frankly, you'd better well be assured in your own mind of your source for the payoff funds because thirty-six months rolls around real fast, and if you don't have the dollars you could be in big trouble.

Relating to mortgages, too, there are even more variables that are up for discussion such as whether the purchase money mortgage is fully amortizing, how the purchase money mortgage payments are to be made (monthly, quarterly, semiannually, or yearly), and if the purchase money mortgage set up on a partially amortizing basis (meaning only *part* of the principal is paid and there is a remaining balloon payment at the end of the term) requires interest only payments (sometimes referred to as a standing mortgage) or amortizing, including regular interest payments.

Other questions for you to negotiate include when and where the closing will take place and which items of personal property go with the sale such as air conditioners, refrigerators, washers and dryers, and so forth.

It's a good idea to write down these different points before you go into negotiations. Give some thought to which of these variables are most important to you and, conversely, which are important to the seller. These variables are like soldiers that you'll be using in your negotiations battle, and you'll want to know at the start which to fight for and which to sacrifice. Seasoned real estate investors go into negotiations with certain areas they're prepared to concede and use as trade-offs to get something they want. In some circles they call these "give-ups" or "front porches." The strategy is to lock onto an area that you know is important to the seller but not necessarily of equal importance to you. For example, as you're shown through the seller's house, you hear the couple refer with pride to their lovely chandelier in the front hallway that they've expressed interest in taking with them. However, you can take it or leave it, but you nonetheless include it as part of your purchase offer along with all the other conditions you're fighting to get. If human nature runs true to course, the sellers will oppose you on the chandelier, and, if you play your cards right, you can keep insisting that the chandelier is part of the deal, finally conceding its ownership to sellers in exchange for something that's really of importance to you.

There are two periods when it would not be to your advantage to enter into serious negotiations. If you're upset about anything because of a loss (real or imagined) of some kind in your business, family, or social life, you'd be well advised to put off negotiations because you will not be at your strongest emotional level. Or, if you're particularly elated about some good fortune that's come your way in another part of your life, then during this period also you will not tend to view things realistically. Negotiations are a battleground, so you have to be at your best physically and mentally. In this same light, seasoned real estate investors, after they've had a closing on a highly profitable sale, know that they're on an emotional high and, equipped with this self-knowledge, will not get involved with another transaction until they've come down to earth.

QUID PRO QUO

Quid pro quo negotiating is a better way to refer to the negotiation process; this Latin phrase means "one thing in return for another." The negotiation process for acquiring a property comprises three stages. Stage One is the initial offer. Stage Two is the counteroffer to the seller's counteroffer. Stage Three is usually where the two parties finally reach a settlement, or not, as the case may be.

In order to get the seller interested in the initial offer, it will have to contain something of value to interest him. It might consist of a high cash down offer and a low total purchase price for the property coupled with small purchase money mortgage from the seller. The seller might like the cash down part of the offer, express unhappiness with the offered price for the property, and say he could "live with" the small, short-term second mortgage. After an appropriate lapse of time the buyer might make a new offer reflecting a higher total price for the property but with less cash down and a slightly larger second mortgage and longer term at a lower interest rate. By now, the sellers are probably hooked. Most sellers have a tremendous drive to see that they get as full a price on their property as possible in order to confirm their self-image as astute businesspersons. Utilize this universal drive of all sellers as a stepping stone to get the most favorable financing. Remember that *conditions of sale are much more important than the price of the sale*.

Subsequent offers and counteroffers will continue to raise the price of the property but lower the cash down commitment and increase the amount of the purchase money mortgage under more favored conditions (that is, the rate of interest and the size of the balloon payment). By the time the negotiations finally close, you may well have bought the property with as little of your own money as possible.

There are several factors that should come into play to make this kind of bargaining successful. First, dealing in need-to-sell situations plays a major role in the effectiveness of these tactics. Also, *all* the offers should have a clause that the offer is subject to advice of counsel. Why? Because if the seller accepts the initial offer with the high cash down payment, the buyer will have no escape clause and will be obliged to go through with the deal. Another important factor is the seller's taking back financing in the form of a purchase money mortgage, because as the buyer cuts down the amount of his cash down payment in subsequent offers, these dollars then are tacked onto the increasing size of the purchase money mortgage. Finally, time itself can be a potent force in your negotiations to be used to your advantage. The time *between* offers and counteroffers ought to be delayed as much as possible so that the seller is hooked into the transaction. Remember, with a need-to-sell situation you're dealing with someone who is anxious to dispose of his property and therefore is very mindful of time, so the reason for pressurizing time is as much a psychological ploy as it is actual demand.

Following is a series of offers planned out *before* the first offer is made. This is a graphic strategy you can use.

Obviously, each stage and each variable element in the stage isn't going to come out *exactly* as you would want, but by preplanning the strategy and roughing in the elements of each subsequent offer, you will more often than not be able to come out close to your ultimate

PROPERTY OFFERED AT: $72,000

1ST OFFER: $58,000	2ND OFFER: $64,000	3RD OFFER: $66,500	4TH OFFER: $68,500
Cash down —$21,000	Cash down —$15,000	Cash down —$ 9,000	Cash down —$ 5,700
1st mortgage from bank —$33,000 purchase money mortgage	1st mortgage from bank —$43,000 purchase money mortgage	1st mortgage from bank —$45,000 purchase money mortgage	1st mortgage from bank —$48,000 purchase money mortgage
from seller —$ 4,000 • payable in 1 year • fully amortizing • 16 percent interest	from seller —$ 8,000 • payable in 3 years • partially amortizing • 13 percent interest	from seller —$12,500 • payable in 4 years • interest only • 12 percent interest	from seller —$14,800 • payable in 5 years • interest only • 9 percent interest

objective: to buy with as little out-of-pocket cash as possible.

When negotiating, try to determine if there is some kind of pattern to the amount of dollars in each subsequent counteroffer by the seller. For example, if two total price reductions are each $1,000, you can pretty well guess a third reduction might be the same and therefore could adopt your negotiating strategy accordingly. The biggest concessions are invariably given in the earliest stages of the negotiations. And, as the negotiating process moves along, each party has a tendency to become more entrenched in his position, probably more for emotional reasons than anything else.

To further your cause, try to bring as many things to bear as possible that will substantiate your position. Anything that will bring credibility, authenticity, or a sense of legitimacy to your position is bound to have some beneficial effect. If you can show the seller something written, especially in printed form, it takes on the aura of Holy Writ. Knowing this, be on the lookout for any articles in newspapers, magazines, newsletters, or the like on how creative financing is becoming an increasingly more acceptable way to sell, how more home sellers are helping in the financing, how sellers can help buyers even to offering to help them at the mortgaging bank (as co-signers or prevailing on the real estate agent to take a promissory note for part or all of his commission), or some other real estate item that might aid your cause.

Of course, the reverse of this approach could be brought into play if the seller is supplying you all kinds of things to justify *his* price. You're certain to be presented with printed matter indicating that buying his house in such a wonderfully appreciating neighborhood is akin to being able to mine your own gold. Do yourself a favor and challenge these and any other statements, credentials, or articles when it's to your advantage.

The trick in much of these negotiations is *caring but not caring too much*—which means wanting to buy the house but not wanting it so much that you can taste it. When you put yourself into that position, then you're too emotionally involved and, as a result, you will probably not make the best deal for yourself. It's only when you can convey a certain indifference as to the final outcome that you will do that much better for yourself in negotiating. If, after all, the broker gets the idea from you, and you in turn are perceived as "wanting the house in the worst way" then, frankly, you'll probably get it in the worst way possible because the broker just might convey your feelings to the seller, and then the seller naturally will begin to take a more rigid position on both his price and conditions. The most important thing that will give you the inner strength not to chase after the property is to have as many *buying options* available to yourself as you can. As mentioned earlier in this book, working with several brokers who bring you several interesting properties will increase your options. After all, there's no law saying you can't make offers on several properties at the same time; just make certain you include a clause making each offer subject to advice of counsel, or use any other "subject to" condition that will give you an opportunity to back out of the deal.

MISCELLANEOUS NEGOTIATING POINTS

Make a list of all the defects in the house or on the grounds. If there are defects in the surrounding neighborhood (its convenience, proximity to your job, shopping, entertainment), then make a note of them too. When you make your initial offer subject to satisfactory licensed inspection, mention at the time a *few* of these defects. However, do not mention *all* the defects at the time of your initial offer because you'll want to save some of them to use when you make your counteroffer, thereby strengthening the effect of the counteroffer. ("Well, we've reviewed our offer, and although we are willing to increase our offer by $1,500 we can't possibly go beyond that, particularly in light of the fact that your garage is not going to be big enough for the new car we've got our eye on. Therefore, we'd have additional expenses to extend. . . .")

Bring out drawbacks to the seller about some aspects of the neighborhood, because this can be an effective bargaining tool. A house defect can always be repaired, but a drawback in the neighborhood is usually insurmountable and uncorrectable. As an example of this in operation, I know an investor who, each time he makes an offer, puts forward another zinger, another blemish or perceived drawback. In so doing, he shakes the seller's confidence a little more. These perceived drawbacks are ammunition for you, too, so space them out in order to get the most leverage out of them.

Another tactic for you to keep in mind is that all bargaining does not have to be in the area of price. *Conditions of sale* are extremely important to the success of your negotiations. Conditions of sale can be used during the negotiating process as trade-off tools to reduce the price of the property. However, after you've been in the negotiation process for a while and you're coming down to the wire with the seller, you may find yourself at a stand-off. What do you do when you've gotten most if not all the conditions of sale you can realistically hope to get, yet the seller is firm at a total price that is above what you're willing to pay. Get your discussions away from price and get your seller to throw in some other *asset* he might have in lieu of the price difference—kind of a, "Well, I can see that you're absolutely firm on your price, which is certainly your privilege, and I in turn am just as firm in my price. In order for us to get this off dead center, I'd like to suggest the following: I'll concede to you and buy at your price if you throw in the Ride 'Em Mower you have sitting in the garage and the snow blower."

Getting the seller to exchange some asset (it could be household equipment, a product, services, or a collectible) in place of a cash reduction of the total price will sometimes loosen the logjam that's developed between you and the seller. It gives the seller a way of saving face and, in turn, it has given you a valuable asset that you can use or convert to cash.

Sometimes, after a long give-and-take exchange on price has taken place and both parties have become entrenched in their positions, the broker will need the patience of a saint, the insight of a mind reader, and the tact and patience of a United Nations representative to get the situation moving again. If the broker can, separately, get each side to start thinking about splitting the difference, he might save the situation and make himself a well-earned commission. "Splitting the difference" is a well-used last-ditch compromise that has

122

moved many a stalled negotiation back into the mainstream and might prove helpful to you in your negotiations.

You might also find it helpful to have a "fall guy." This is the person (real or a figment of your imagination) who you tell the seller you have to confer with before you can proceed. Then, having bought yourself extra time for additional consideration or strategic stalling, you can always come back with, "Gee, I'm sorry, but my Uncle Louie doesn't think that's such a good deal for me." You may have already run into this kind of negotiating tactic but may not have recognized it. It goes something like this: "I understand your position, but I don't think our board of directors would go along with it," or "I took your offer on the car back to the sales manager and he says he'd love to have you own this car but you'll have to do a little better if you want to buy this beauty," or "If it were up to me, I'd say okay, but you know how your mother feels about these kinds of things."

Get yourself a fall guy and let him be the bad guy, not you. Sometimes when a buyer is negotiating with *two* sophisticated owners, the sellers will have preplanned the negotiations by having one of them purposely play the mean guy who becomes your adversary, and the other becoming the nice guy, almost to the point that he's psychologically joining forces with you to protect you. Keep your guard up because it's all a game and the other side will be doing its share of trying to "psych you out" just as you are trying to make a favorable deal on your behalf. Frankly, the best deals are the ones where both sides feel satisfied with the final results rather than where one side tries to blast the other side off the map and leave the adversary a bloody mess. Even if a general sense of fair play didn't dictate that the other side should also be left feeling satisfied, remember that some day, either directly or indirectly, your paths may cross again and it's better to leave them smiling and thinking well of you than frowning and speaking ill of you.

In essence, the man who drives the hard bargain and tries to get the last drop of blood isn't the best negotiator. In fact, this kind of person will invariably stimulate a combative and argumentative response that will probably make you say, "Hey, I'll show this guy a thing or two. He's not going to push me around!" The old saw is still true: You catch more flies with honey than you do with vinegar. If the other side perceives you as generally reasonable and understanding of their needs, then they will take a more cooperative, sympathetic, and open approach to *your* needs. As a result there will be a mutual area of trust, with both sides willing to make concessions in order to meet a common goal. When you run into roadblocks, you have to come up with fair alternatives. If you go into battle with the "I have to win at all costs" attitude, there's a good chance that negotiations will never come to a satisfactory conclusion. On the other hand, if you're willing to make concessions in order to receive concessions and you are able to think creatively of alternative approaches when logjams arise, then chances are you'll have fruitful negotiations. Let the other party know that you're interested in his problems. You will find that the other party is usually less defensive when he sees that you're not trying to jam your demands down his throat and are not interested in debating everything, but are trying to identify problems and work them out.

If you're the type that's not particularly interested in going through all these negotiating tactics and the trials and tribulations that accompany them, don't despair. You can always hire someone to handle your negotia-

124

tions for you. The fee for such services can be a fixed amount of cash or a prearranged percentage. The most logical sources for someone to represent you might be an attorney, particularly a real estate lawyer; an experienced businessman who has had a depth of sales or labor negotiating experience; a real estate investor experienced in buying or selling properties; or a retired businessperson who has had experience in dealing with people and business demands.

You need to present your personal position in all transactions, whether you choose to handle it yourself or authorize someone else to represent you. It is not enough for you to turn this area completely over to a real estate broker and ask him to buy you a house at a good price and on good conditions of sale. Such an arrangement is impractical for all parties concerned and a foolish abdication of your responsibility to yourself.

A FEW FINAL POINTS

1. Try to do your negotiating on *your* turf, not on the other party's.

2. Don't negotiate on the phone, as you'll want to watch for facial, eye, or body reaction to your point. Remember, too, it's easier for someone to say no over the phone than it is in person.

3. Don't be belligerent or critical of the other person. You'll get better results if the other person likes you.

4. Try to keep your discussion based on the issues, not on personalities.

5. Write down concessions as they are made in the course of the negotiations so that you have a clear written record of what was agreed upon.

6. If you run into a negative response to your offer, this only means that the other party is looking for different solutions to the problem. Don't take the no as a rejection, but rather as a signpost that says, "Please take another road."

7. Use some of your concessions in the beginning in order to get the proceedings off to a cooperative start. Later on in the negotiations, concessions can be given in smaller increments as things get tougher near the end.

8. When you've reached as far as you can go, don't blurt out an abrasive ultimatum such as, "That's as far as I can go; take it or leave it." Rather, say something to the effect that "I'd love to be in a position to offer you more, but I just can't afford to go beyond this point."

If you do your homework, try to fulfill the needs of the other party, and act in a cooperative way, using some of the common-sense tactics we've covered in this chapter, there's a strong chance you not only will wind up with a negotiated house purchase to your liking but will have saved yourself thousands of out-of-pocket dollars. And that's the name of the game!

CHAPTER SEVEN

HOW TO SAVE YOURSELF CASH BY KNOWING ABOUT MORTGAGES

Upheaval has to be the most suitable word to describe what's happened in the conventional residential mortgage market recently as conventional lending sources such as thrift institutions, savings banks, and commercial banks have all moved into gear with an entire smorgasbord of new and different mortgage instruments. They are all structured to keep the lender's money profitable or fluid in an ever-changing money market. Frankly, when it comes to money matters in the 80's, the only thing that you can really count on is that there *will* be change. Not since the late 20's, when mortgage lenders finally dropped the use of the onerous short-term balloon mortgage and adopted the long-term (25- to 30-year) fully amortizing mortgage, has there been anything as revolutionary as the current movement away from fixed-rate mortgages into a variety of variable interest rate mortgage programs. On reflection, this movement was inevitable, because borrowing money on a short fixed-rate basis which is what a bank does when it "borrows" money from depositors in the form of high interest rate Certificates of Deposit and other instruments, and then turning around and loaning it out long (20- to 30-years) at a fixed rate, has got to be crap-shooting carried to a high degree. In previous years, the cost of money was more constant, and borrowing short and lending long at fixed rates was acceptable. However, since the early 70's and with the advent of heated infla-tion, a continuation of this policy would spell financial disaster to any lender. Hence, the urgent need by banks to move into more fluid mortgage instruments with variable rates that can adjust to the ever-changing costs of money.

From your point of view as a borrower, the introduction of these variable-rate mortgage programs means two things. First, lenders will have at their disposal a means by which to offer mortgages. Without the introduction of the variable interest rate concept all mortgage funds available for loans would dry up. Second, the borrower (the mort-gagor) is now asked to share in the risk with the lender (mortgagee). Unlike a fixed-rate long-term mortgage where you knew you had a constant interest rate cost, the variable-interest mortgage rates go up or down as the rate is adjusted according to the cost of money to the bank.

The variable interest rate concept can be a plus or a minus for the borrower. At this writing, with home mort-gage interest rates at 17 to 18 percent and up, lending officials claim that a current variable interest rate mortgage can be to the borrower's advantage because, as money rates come down, the variable interest rate mortgage costs to the borrower will also be adjusted downward.

On the other side of the coin is the fact that today's variable interest rate borrower is now sharing the move-ment of money costs with the bank. It is a risk factor that previously was resident with the lender only and considered part of the risk–reward balance inherent in lending. It would be nice but wishful thinking if the borrower received some benefit for his now having to share the risk factor in a mortgage based on its fluctuating interest costs, but it isn't so. The rebuttal that the borrower will derive the benefit when the interest rate subsides is nice to think about, too, but over the long range rates seem to be moving up.

What it boils down to is that variable interest rate mortgages may some day become the only game in town. Although fixed-rate mortgages are not yet completely dead, they are at best comatose. (However, don't write them off too quickly. They've been around a long time and they're not going to completely disappear overnight with consumer interest in them continuing.) If you have the opportunity to choose between a fixed-rate mortgage and a variable interest rate mortgage, you will have to weigh the advantages and disadvantages of both on a short-term and long-term basis. As an example, recently I received both a fixed-rate and variable-rate quotation from a federally chartered savings and loan association in New England as follows:

	FIXED-RATE MORTGAGE	VARIABLE-RATE MORTGAGE
Loan:	80 percent of appraised value	80 percent of appraised value
Interest rate:	17.5 percent	17 percent—adjusted once a year with no cap†
Points:*	3 points	2 points
Prepayment penalty:	5 years	None

* A point is a one-time charge that is equal to one percentage point of the amount of the mortgage. Example: 3 points on a $50,000 mortgage would equal $1,500 (3 percent × $50,000 = $1,500).
† *No cap* indicates that the lender does not have a limit as to how far he can adjust upward or downward in the interest rate as it relates to whatever index is being used.

If you had been offered these two alternative programs, several considerations might pass through your mind:

1) How much of a factor to me is the additional expense of an extra point (that is, 3 points on a fixed-rate mortgage versus 2 points on a variable mortgage)? Is it something that I can handle?

2) Would I be moving from or selling the house within the five-year prepayment penalty period and, if so, how much of a factor would the prepayment penalty cost be to me?

3) Could I handle additional increased mortgage payments if the variable-rate mortgage called for higher costs to me? How much higher? For how long? What does my job or financial future look like over the short term (one to three years), and the long term (five to ten years)? Are interest rates going up or down, and for how long?

What you can surmise from all this is that the lenders who are interested in promoting their variable-rate mortgages are betting that inflation will be with us for a long time. The lender offering fixed-rate mortgages is expecting inflation and interest rates to decline. And the lender offering both kinds of programs is probably trying to cover all possible bases. An interesting thought to keep in mind is that it wasn't the customers who decided that traditional one-rate loans weren't good enough.

As a mortgage borrower today, you'll have to learn to play many roles. You'll have to be part crystal ball reader, part soothsayer, part financial investment expert, and part psychiatrist, the last in order to be able to cope with your emotional ups and downs as your financial picture changes along with a multitude of financial factors outside your control. At least you can save money in one area: You won't have to go to the horse races for financial excitement; just stay inside your mortgaged home and wait with bated breath to see if, for the rate adjustment period coming up, you're going to be a winner (if the rate stays the same or goes down) or a loser (if the rate goes up).

Each mortgage borrower will have to establish for himself whether he can financially handle possible future upward interest rate adjustments. As a possible insight as to how these upward interest rate adjustments might affect your monthly mortgage payments, following is an example of a schedule that one federally chartered savings and loan shows to prospective borrowers so they can better understand the concept of a variable interest rate mortgage (also called "adjustable mortgage loan," or AML).

An example of how your AML works

The following shows what could happen over a two-year period to an adjustable mortgage loan.

The example assumes:

Loan amount:	$50,000
Loan term:	30 years
Contract interest rate:	16.00%(Closing date December 15, 1980)
Initial payment:	$672.38(First payment due January 1, 1981)
Initial index value:	14.50%

First Rate and Payment Adjustment	March 1, 1982 (Assume new index 15.50%)
Second Rate and Payment Adjustment	March 1, 1983 (Assume new index 14.00%)
Payment Adjustment Notice Sent	February 1, 1982, and February 1, 1983

MONTH	INDEX VALUE	INDEX CHANGE	INTEREST RATE	PAYMENT	LOAN BALANCE
January 1981	14.50%		16.00%	$672.38	$49,994.29
February			16.00	672.38	49,988.50
March			16.00	672.38	49,982.63
April			16.00	672.38	49,976.68
May			16.00	672.38	49,970.66
June			16.00	672.38	49,964.55
July			16.00	672.38	49,583.37
August			16.00	672.38	49,952.10
September			16.00	672.38	49,945.74
October			16.00	672.38	49,939.31
November			16.00	672.38	49,932.78
December			16.00	672.38	49,926.17
January 1982			16.00	672.38	49,919.48
February			16.00	672.38	49,912.69
March	15.50%	+1.00%	17.00	712.58	49,907.21
April			17.00	712.58	49,901.64
May			17.00	712.58	49,896.00
June			17.00	712.58	49,890.28
July			17.00	712.58	49,884.48
August			17.00	712.58	49,878.60
September			17.00	712.58	49,872.63
October			17.00	712.58	49,866.58
November			17.00	712.58	49,860.44
December			17.00	712.58	49,854.21
January 1982			17.00	712.58	49,847.90
February			17.00	712.58	49,841.50
March	14.00%	− .50%	15.50	652.76	49,832.53

INTEREST RATE ADJUSTMENT

On the interest adjustment data, the new interest rate on your loan will be equal to the original contract rate plus the difference between the initial index value and the index value most recently available as of the date of notification, for example the most recent index value for the March 1982 rate adjustment is 15.50%. This is plus 1.00% increase over the original index value of 14.50%. Therefore, the new interest rate in effect for this loan for March 1982 to February 1983 will be 17% (16.00% + 1.00% = 17.00%).

I/we acknowledge receipt of the above AML disclosure and a separate example of the operation of the type of AML to be offered to us.

_____   _____
        Signature   Signature
                   Borrower

Because variable-rate mortgages are still relatively new in the mortgage market and have not been field-tested over an extensive period of years, it's fair to assume that as political or consumer reactions come on-stream, various terms or conditions of these adjustable-rate mortgage programs may be modified in the future. Because of this possibility, you should keep yourself posted and make your mortgage decisions based on the variable-rate mortgage information you get at the time you apply for a mortgage loan. Outdated mortgage information might be misleading, so make sure your information is current.

Because there may be variations from state to state in the terms and conditions of these variable-rate programs, you should keep yourself updated on what's available to you in these mortgage programs in the town or state you're interested in.

As we've said throughout this book, do your home-work. In the mortgage area this means you must shop around to as many different lenders as you can in order to see what different kinds of mortgage programs (fixed-rate mortgages or variable-rate mortgages) are available. What you're trying to do is educate yourself as thoroughly and as quickly as you can in order to make the most beneficial decision for yourself. Talk to lenders and knowledgeable real estate brokers in the community in order to get as broad a base as possible of different mortgage programs to choose from. Call four to six

IMPORTANT INFORMATION ABOUT THE ADJUSTABLE MORTGAGE LOAN
PLEASE READ CAREFULLY

You have received an application form for an adjustable loan ("AML"). The AML may differ from other mortgages with which you are familiar.

General Description of Adjustable Mortgage Loan

The adjustable mortgage loan is a flexible instrument. Its interest rate may be adjusted by the lender from time to time. Such adjustments will result in increases or decreases in your payment amount, in the outstanding principal loan balance, in the loan term, or in all three (see discussion below relating to these types of adjustments). Federal regulations place no limit on the amount by which the interest-rate may be adjusted either at any one time or over the life of the loan, or on the frequency with which it may be adjusted. Adjustments to the interest rate must reflect the movement of a single, specified index. This does not mean that the particular loan agreement you sign must, by law, permit unlimited interest rate changes. It merely means that, if you desire to have certain rate-adjustment limitations placed in your loan agreement, that is a matter you should negotiate with the lender. You may also want to make inquiries concerning loan terms offered by other lenders on AMLs to compare the terms and conditions.

Another flexible feature of the AML is that the regular payment amount may be increased or decreased by the lender from time to time to reflect changes in the interest rate. Again, Federal regulations place no limitations on the amount by which the lender may adjust payments at any one time, or on the frequency of payment adjustments. If you wish to have particular provisions in your loan agreement regarding adjustments to the payment amount, you should negotiate such terms with the lender.

A third flexible feature of the AML is that the outstanding principal loan balance (the total amount you owe) may be increased or decreased from time to time when, because of adjustments to the interest rate, the payment amount is either too small to cover interest due on the loan, or larger than is necessary to pay off the loan over the remaining term of the loan.

The final flexible feature of the AML is that the loan term may be lengthened or shortened from time to time, corresponding to an increase or decrease in the interest rate. When the term is extended in connection with a rate increase, the payment amount does not have to be increased to the same extent as if the term had not been lengthened. In no case may the total term of the loan exceed 40 years.

The combination of these four basic features allows an association to offer a variety of mortgage loans. For example, one type of loan could permit rate adjustments with corresponding changes in the payment amount. Alternatively, a loan could permit rate adjustments to occur more frequently than payment adjustments, limit the amount by which the payment could be adjusted, and/or provide for corresponding adjustments to the principal loan balance.

Index

Adjustments to the interest rate of an AML must correspond directly to the movement of an index, subject to such rate-adjustment limitations as may be contained in the loan contract. If the index has moved down, the lender must reduce the interest rate by at least the decrease in the index. If the index has moved up, the lender has the right to increase the interest rate by that amount. Although taking such an increase is optional by the lender, you should be aware that the lender has this right and may become contractually obligated to exercise it.

DESCRIPTION OF THE INDEX TO BE USED _____

DATE OF INITIAL INDEX VALUE _____ , 19___ .

INITIAL INDEX VALUE (IF KNOWN) _____

SOURCE(S) WHERE THE INDEX MAY BE READILY OBTAINED _____

HIGH AND LOW POINTS ON THE INDEX THE PREVIOUS CALENDAR YEAR: High _____ Low _____

KEY TERMS OF _____ ADJUSTABLE MORTGAGE LOAN

Following is a summary of the basic terms on the type of AML to be offered to you. This summary is intended for reference purposes only. Important information relating specifically to your loan will be contained in the loan agreement.

Loan Term _____ years

Frequency of Rate Changes _____ months

Frequency of Payment Changes _____ months

Maximum Rate Changes @ One Time _____ % ☐ Not Applicable

Maximum Rate Change Over the Life of the Loan _____ % ☐ Not Applicable

Maximum Payment Change @ One Time _____ % ☐ Not Applicable

Minimum Rate Increment _____ % ☐ Not Applicable

Possible Adjustments to Principal Loan Balance ☐ Yes ☐ No

How Your Adjustable Mortgage Loan Would Work

The initial interest rate offered by _____ on your AML will be established and disclosed to you on _____ based on the market conditions at the time.

All payment changes are based on changes in the rate or value of the Index selected for your AML. Rate changes may cause a payment change or they may result in a longer loan term or a possible change in the principal loan balance. The box(es) checked below will reflect the basic operation of your AML.

☐ Your loan term may either be shortened, or be extended, up to total loan term of 40 years, to partially offset a payment change increase.

☐ Your monthly payment will remain fixed for _____ months. Rate changes that occur during this fixed period may increase or decrease the principal loan balance. Payment changes will be made to amortize your AML over the remaining term at the end of each fixed period.

☐ All rate changes will result in a corresponding payment change, subject to the terms stated above for rate change increases, but no limitation for rate change decreases.

☐ Your payment change will have a "cap" or limit of _____% per rate change increase. Rate change increases might exceed the payment change "cap" causing increases in the principal loan amount through "negative amortization." There's no limitation for rate change decreases.

☐

_____
_____
_____
_____

Notice of Payment Adjustments

_____ will send you notice of an adjustment to the payment amount at least 30 but not more than 45 days before it becomes effective. The notice will contain the following information:

1. The fact that the payment on the loan with the association, secured by a mortgage or deed of trust on property located at the appropriate address, is scheduled to be adjusted on a particular date;

2. The outstanding balance of the loan, on the adjustment date, assuming timely payment of the remaining payments due by that date;

3. The interest rate on the loan as of the adjustment date, the index value on which that interest rate will be in effect, the next following payment adjustment date, and the rate adjustment dates, if any, between the upcoming payment adjustment date and the next following payment adjustment date;

4. The payment amount as of the payment adjustment date;

5. The date(s), if any, on which the rate was adjusted since the last payment adjustment, the rates on each such rate adjustment date, and the index values corresponding to each such date;

6. The dates, if any, on which the outstanding principal loan balance was adjusted since the last payment adjustment, and the net change in the outstanding principal loan balance since the last payment adjustment;

7. The fact that the borrower may pay off the entire loan or part of it without penalty at any time; and

8. The title and telephone number of an association employee who can answer questions about the notice

Prepayment Penalty

You may prepay an AML in whole or in part without penalty at any time during the term of the loan.

Fees

You will be charged fees by _____ and other persons in connection with the origination of your AML. The association will give you an estimate of these fees after receiving your loan application. However, you will not be charged any costs or fees in connection with any regularly-scheduled adjustment to the interest rate, the payment, the outstanding principal loan balance, or the loan term initiated by the lender.

I/We acknowledge receipt of the above AML disclosure and a separate example of the operation of the type of AML to be offered to us.

_____
Signature

_____
Signature

local institutions and ask about terms. Include in your survey commercial banks, savings and loan associations, and, if they exist in your region, mutual savings banks. The variety of rates and terms offered by different institutions in the same locality is the greatest in recent history, and the cost of a few phone calls can bring savings in the thousands of dollars.

At the core of this advice is a concept that may be new to first-time home buyers or those who are uninitiated in the ways of finance: Banks and lenders have a product called money that they are selling. If you do comparative shopping for food and clothing check out different stores before you make your final decision, then apply this same principle when you go shopping for a mortgage loan. Even the Federal National Mortgage Association (Fannie Mae), a congressionally chartered but privately owned and operated corporation that is one of the country's largest secondary purchasers of mortgages, offers the same kind of advice to home buyers faced with the complexities of adjustable-rate mortgages for the first time. Shop around!

Adjustable-rate plans vary greatly from lender to lender, community to community, and state to state. Therefore, you'll have to study the differences in the terms and conditions. For example, rate adjustments are made at regular intervals, sometimes ranging from every six months to upwards of every five years. Also, the index used to establish the interest rate can be tied to short-term interest rates, such as six-month treasury bills, or to longer-term rates, such as five-year treasury bills.

Where your personal finances and income are today and what they will be down the road have to play an important role in your personal decision as to whether you go with a fixed-rate or a variable-rate mortgage, assuming both types of programs are available. Naturally, a fixed-rate mortgage (if you can get one and can handle the initial higher interest rate) is preferable, if you can live with the prepayment penalty clause (which, depending upon the mortgage, will usually run for up to 3 years or up to 5 years). If rates were to come down enough to justify the closing costs, you could get a new, lower-rated mortgage and pay off your higher-rated mortgage and you therefore would not be subject to the potentially higher interest rates that just might be down the road. Who knows? Ten years from now people may be looking back nostalgically at the 80's and saying, "Boy, remember the good old days when you could still get a fixed interest rate long-term mortgage in the 14 to 18 percent range!"

If you and I knew with certainty where inflation and interest rates will be down the road, we could do financial wonders for ourselves! However, without this kind of clairvoyance, we all have to use our own good judgment. Therefore, don't be too quick to buy as gospel the words of any one expert or lender or author in this area. Get as much input as you can from as many intelligent sources as you can, and then, when you've weighed all the facts and conjectures, follow your own good instincts. As the old saying goes, "Yesterday is always the best time to buy real estate."

Here are some other questions to think about when considering and comparing specific adjustable-rate mortgages. How often will the rate move? Is there a maximum limit on each rate change? How much can the rate change over the term of the loan? What index will be used?

TYPES OF MORTGAGES

CONVENTIONAL MORTGAGE

This is the traditional, longstanding type of mortgage that most people are familiar with. It has a fixed-interest rate and it is usually issued for a 25- to 30-year period. Because the interest rate stays the same over the life of the loan, the total monthly payment of principal and interest remains constant. Although these loans are still available in some areas, in all likelihood you will probably be paying a higher interest rate in exchange for the complete assurance of level monthly payments. If you feel you can handle the different cost factors in this kind of fixed-rate mortgage versus the variable-rate mortgage, and if you feel that inflation is going to be around for a while, conventional financing might be the way for you to go. With the fixed-rate conventional mortgage, down payment requirements can range from under 20 percent to more than 20 percent. When the rate is under 20 percent, some lenders require the borrower to buy private mortgage insurance in order to protect the lender in case the borrower defaults on his loan.

Criteria for whether the lender will make the mortgage loan vary from bank to bank, but most lenders are interested in the prospective borrower's credit history, employment stability and future prospects, assets (liquid and nonliquid), the appraisal report on the property, and the amount of loan requested in relationship to the appraised value of the house. The latter is sometimes referred to as the loan-to-value ratio. For example, an 80 percent loan-to-value ratio means that the lender would extend a loan of 80 percent of the bank's appraised value of the house: if a bank appraised a house at $70,000, they would extend up to a $56,000 mortgage ($70,000 times .80 = $56,000).

The lender will take into consideration your current income, too. A general rule of thumb used by some lenders is that your monthly housing expenses (mortgage payments, taxes and insurance, but not including utilities) should not exceed 25 to 28 percent of your gross monthly income. Another rule of thumb: potential lenders will consider a mortgage amount equal to approximately 1½ times your income. Thus, if you make $30,000, a $45,000 mortgage might be in the ball park.

Other factors may also come into play particularly in tight money times: if you're currently a customer of the bank; how long a time have you been a customer; how important a customer are you; to what extent do you use the bank's services; can you be instrumental in bringing additional customers to the bank.

VA LOANS

Veteran Administration (VA) loans are offered only to those persons with military service. Local VA offices will be able to supply you with all the specific requirements needed to qualify for this kind of mortgage. Though VA loans are backed by the government, they are obtained from local private lenders. As a general rule the interest rate on these kinds of loans will be lower than current mortgage rates. However, lenders will charge points to the seller as well as an origination fee of 1 percent of the loan in order to compensate them for the lower interest rate. The seller, when he's dealing with a VA mortgage buyer, knows he's going to have to pay points. He probably wants those extra dollars to originate with the buyer. Therefore, low interest rate

VA mortgage benefits may be somewhat diluted by a seller wanting more dollars for himself.

A VA mortgage usually requires more time to process than a conventional mortgage. A conventional mortgage might take three to five weeks for the paperwork, whereas an FHA or VA mortgage might take eight weeks. Therefore, if a speedy closing is of major importance to you, you may have to examine this aspect closely to see if it's worthwhile.

However, VA loans are assumable; when you've bought with this kind of mortgage and later you're ready to sell, this assumable VA mortgage could be an important, marketable asset for you as you trade up to your next home.

With a VA mortgage, if you're an honorably discharged veteran and you meet all their requirements, you can get 100 percent mortgage financing up to $110,000, with nothing down, to buy a 1- to 4-family house to be owner-occupied by you. If the house you want to buy costs more than $110,000, many lenders will ask that you make a cash down payment. In both cases, your income would have to be sufficient to support the loan payments.

FHA LEVEL-PAYMENT LOANS

FHA (Federal Housing Administration) loans are available to *any* qualified buyer through local lenders that offer FHA financing. FHA, like VA mortgages, usually have lower than the prevailing interest rates; however, this advantage is usually offset by the payment of points. An FHA loan, like a VA loan, is government-backed, and the government periodically sets the interest rates. Unlike a VA loan (available only to qualified veterans), an FHA loan is available to anyone who qualifies as to income, length and type of employment, credit standing, etc.

The FHA down payment requirements are 3 percent of the first $25,000 and 5 percent of the remaining amount, with a maximum loan usually of $67,500. In areas with higher housing costs loans can escalate to $90,000. In order to get more information about the loan limits in your area, you should contact the local FHA office.

If local lenders in your community do not offer VA or FHA mortgage loans, you can touch base with private mortgage lending firms, such as Lomas & Nettleson, who are active throughout the country offering government-backed mortgage programs, as well as conventional mortgages. If you qualify, a VA mortgage might be a better deal for you because you'd be getting 100 percent financing, with no cash down, whereas with an FHA loan there are cash down requirements plus points.

FHA GRADUATED MORTGAGE PAYMENT PROGRAM

Under this mortgage payment arrangement, where it's assumed the borrower will be making more income in future years, earlier monthly mortgage payments will be less costly than in a traditionally structured level-payment program. With this *graduated* mortgage payment program, the interest rate will usually be half a percentage point more than with a level-payment program, but your monthly mortgage payments will cost you approximately 18 to 20 percent less. Payments increase for a number of years according to a schedule, eventually leveling out at an amount higher than it would be with a level-payment plan, and there are a number of payment schedules from which you can choose.

GRADUATED PAYMENT CONVENTIONAL MORTGAGES

Conventionally financed graduated payment mortgages (GPM) are being offered by many lenders today under a variety of names and might warrant your attention. This is particularly true if you're pretty well assured that your income, although limited currently, has encouraging prospects.

The graduated payment mortgage program was designed for the borrower whose current income is less than his financial prospects in the future. Obviously there's some degree of risk here if the future earning power of the buyer does not occur as anticipated. Although the interest rate and the rate of increase on these mortgages is fixed at its origination for the term of the loan, the borrower's monthly payments vary, beginning low and gradually increasing. After five or ten years, depending on what kind of program the lender offers, monthly payments reach a maximum level that is slightly above the level of conventional loans. They remain constant thereafter, and limitations on the rate increases will be stipulated in the mortgage contract.

Under this kind of mortgage program, negative amortization in the early years is taking place, a fancy term that means the monthly payments cover interest only. Thus the borrower's *equity* in the property actually declines temporarily, unless the *market value* of the property increases at least as much as the negative amortization. In inflationary times with well-selected property, this could be a distinct possibility. With the graduated payment mortgage, many individuals who might not be able to afford conventional fixed-interest payments are able to secure a home mortgage. These borrowers are liable for a mortgage balance that is temporarily *grow-*

ing, in contrast to a conventional mortgage loan, whereby the balance would be decreasing.

Both fixed- and variable-rate GPM's are currently being offered by lenders. Most borrowers prefer the fixed-rate form because it allows for increases in payments to be established when the mortgage is originated. In the variable-rate form, adjustments in the interest rate may in turn increase, therefore, or reduce the amount by which the payments may be adjusted. This factor might prove troublesome for some borrowers if interest rates rise at the same time a payment increase is also scheduled.

FLEXIBLE LOAN INSURANCE PROGRAM (FLIP)

The FLIP (flexible loan insurance program) mortgage is another form of the graduated payment plan. It uses the buyer's down payment to ease monthly payments during the first five years. Part or all of the down payment is put into a pledged savings account held by the lender, and a portion is withdrawn to supplement monthly payments. This approach avoids the problem of negative amortization referred to above.

SHARED APPRECIATION MORTGAGES (SAM)

The Shared Appreciation Mortgage is a mortgage loan whereby the home buyer receives an interest rate that is *under* the current market rate, and in return, upon sale of the home or at some other prearranged date the home owner must give the lender a portion (usually a third) of any appreciation on the property's equity. With this kind of program, the loan might have an interest rate of about one third less than the current mortgage interest

145

rate, but the additional appreciation in value is payable whenever the loan becomes due or is paid off.

An equity participation mortgage such as a SAM program might be of interest to the first-time home buyer who can't get into the home ownership market without a lower-than-prevailing rate of interest. For years, large real estate investors, dealing with major income-producing projects, have gotten mortgage loans from insurance companies with conditions not dissimilar to this shared-equity concept that SAM offers for single-family home ownership.

In a shared appreciation mortgage program, after a number of years, usually no more than ten, the interest rate on the mortgage rises to the full current rate and the borrower must then pay the lender's share of the house's capital appreciation, as determined by a mutually acceptable appraiser. The owner can raise the money to pay off the bank by refinancing the mortgage, if necessary.

The SAM concept started in Florida, moved to California, and is gaining acceptance in different parts of the country. As with all these new kinds of mortgage programs, it's best to do your own investigation on the local level to find the variations in the general concept *before* you commit yourself.

VARIABLE-RATE MORTGAGES (VRM)

Another new basic type of mortgage loan comes in a variety of forms and names; it might be called adjustable-rate, variable-rate, or renegotiatable rate mortgages. Basically, all these mortgage loans are similar in that interest rates are not fixed but will go up or down over the term of the loan, within stated limitations regulated by state or federal banking regulations. The amount of the adjustment depends upon changes in prevailing interest rates and/or the financial index used by the lender.

For example, a renegotiable rate mortgage (RRM) plan would offer an interest rate usually somewhat lower than a conventional fixed-rate mortgage loan with the stipulation that its rate could go down if market rates go down. Conversely, it would increase if market rates increase. Rate changes can be made every three years with increases or decreases of no more than 1½ percent during that time. Once the rate is set, it's guaranteed for three years. And, over the 30-year life of a loan the increase or decrease is limited to 5 percent.

Another kind of mortgage started in California and has now spread throughout the country. On this kind, the lender reserves the right to adjust the mortgage interest rate, but this change can be made usually no more than once a year. This type of variable-rate mortgage, however, has fewer limits on the lender and more danger for the borrower. For example, the lender could change the interest rate by, say, 6% if the index used increased by 6% since the date of the last rate change. The amount of change in the rate of interest is subject to the movement of a national index which, in turn, is the average cost of funds for savings and loan associations across the country. When a rate increase is announced to a borrower, he may request that the loan maturity be extended in order to offset the increase in payments. However, the benefit to the borrower of doing this is slim because most of the payments in the early years, particularly in a long-term 30-year mortgage, *are for interest* and not principal, which is the amount that *would* be affected by extending the length of time of the mortgage.

Faced with a possible interest-rate increase, a borrower could also explore the current mortgage market at that time with the idea of refinancing, that is, finding a new mortgage source with a lower interest rate and taking out a new mortgage to pay off the older mortgage. Prepayment penalties and closing costs would have to be analyzed carefully to evaluate if this is a practical means to circumvent the interest rate increase on the existing mortgage.

Graduated mortgage programs, equity participation mortgage programs, adjustable-rate programs such as the variable-rate program and the renegotiable-rate mortgage, and the reverse annuity mortgage (whereby those who have already paid off their mortgage can borrow against the equity in the house) are part of an extensive list of alternatives. There are other concepts also being explored, such as longer terms of 40 years or more in order to bring down the amount of the monthly mortgage payment, and balloon mortgages that require the payment of only interest and that schedule payments in such a way that when the mortgage matures there is still a balance or a "balloon" to pay.

If you've got your eye on a house that you're serious about and if the bank that has the mortgage on it is still sitting with a low interest below the current rate, the bank might want to work out an arrangement whereby you can take over the mortgage at a new blended interest rate. A new rate that is somewhere between the old low rate and the higher current rates can be achieved. However, if the bank senses that you really want to buy the property under any circumstances, then obviously it will have less inducement to work out a modified mortgage arrangement. So be wary and play your cards close to the vest. If the bank senses in you an opportunity to *improve* its mortgage portfolio by getting out of a low interest rate mortgage and getting it increased to a higher, blended rate you might be able to do some good for yourself. An exploratory visit to the bank certainly won't hurt. Remember, "Care enough but not too much." It's when you care *too* much that you get hurt, because then your emotions get in the way of your making the best dollar and cents deal for yourself.

Remember, there is an element of risk in a commitment with a fluctuating rate. Carefully consider how you'll be affected, especially your ability to cope with an upward interest rate adjustment. The prospective home buyer has to have a greater level of knowledge and sophistication about these areas now than when the lenders were offering only the standard 30-year fixed-interest mortgage. In a sense, you and the lender are in a financial game. The variable-rate mortgage programs are basically a gamble on which way interest rates will go. Some people might feel that the lenders have more expertise than the average consumer in this regard. If this is so, it behooves you to make haste slowly and to take your time and check thoroughly the different types of adjustable-rate programs offered.

SUMMARY

First, *even before* considering these different types of mortgage programs, try to avail yourself of a seller's own first mortgage that already exists on the property. Consider if it's assumable or if you can buy subject to it, and if you can use a wraparound mortgage or work out a blended rate with a new modified mortgage program.

You might try to find a property that's free and clear so you can work out a mortgage program with the seller himself taking back a first mortgage against the property, plus any other secondary financing you can work out.

See if you can get the seller to take back a sizeable second mortgage with as long a pay-back–payoff schedule as possible. Be leery of secondary financing where you have a balloon payment due in under five years; those kinds of balloons can explode right in your face. The larger the purchase money mortgage the seller will go along with, the less need you'll have for any of the variable-rate mortgage programs. Remember, favorable secondary financing comes from need-to-sell situations that create the kind of climate where you can get the anxious seller out from under his property and get yourself a home of your own with acceptable deferred financing arrangements. Frankly, if the financial arrangements are not acceptable to you, don't buy. If you don't like the deal when going *into* it, chances are you're not going to be much more enthused with questionable financing arrangements once you own the property and you're faced with those payments as they come due.

If you will be working with one of the types of adjustable-rate mortgage programs outlined, here are a couple of thoughts to keep in mind:

1. Shop. Check out different lenders and different programs offered in the community of your choice. They may vary in both the type of programs offered and the conditions offered.

2. Try to get a handle on what effect rate changes will have on your monthly mortgage payments, and/or look at any projected interest rate schedules the lender might have to show you. Remember that if inflation persists at a high rate with corresponding high interest rates, your adjustable-rate mortgage will be affected accordingly.

3. Look more kindly to the S & L or bank that offers you the best combination of the longest period of *guar-*

anteed monthly payments (that is, without an upward rate adjustment), the least amount of points, and the lowest initial interest rate.

4. Look with favor to the lender who offers the lowest possible upward rate adjustment. You obviously don't want to be hit with a big rate adjustment in your mortgage payments.

5. See if the lending bank offers any other services that might be of interest to you, like favorable checking account services, savings programs, different kinds of personal or business loan programs. Try to get a feeling of whether it's the kind of bank that will work with you if, and when, you call upon it with other dealings.

We're in an entirely new type of mortgage market these days. You've got your work cut out for you to explore and compare the different types of programs that might be available, but your research time could be time well spent because a prudent decision on your part could save you thousands of dollars over the length of the mortgage.

Good hunting!

CHAPTER EIGHT

HOW TO PUT IT ALL TOGETHER WITHOUT GOING BROKE

As difficult and seemingly unaffordable as housing is in today's market, there are nonetheless different kinds of strategies that are being successfully used to get people into homes of their own. These tactics are at their best when you are dealing with need-to-sell situations. The important thing to keep in mind is that these strategies have been proven in the field and have been used in today's market by others whose home-buying problems were probably not much different from yours.

The home buyer of today has to take a completely different attitude than his counterpart a decade ago. The drastic changes in prices and financing have created a need for major changes on the part of the home buyers. It seems like only yesterday when a couple looking for a house and a mortgage had no more to do than drive around with a broker, select a nice, moderately priced home in an acceptable neighborhood, and make a trip down to their local bank to apply for and get a reasonable mortgage. That clear-cut 1-2-3 home-buying process is now, for the vast majority of Americans, a part of history, with little chance that it will ever return. Accepting these facts is the first step for any potential home buyers in today's market if they are to be successful purchasers. And with the acceptance of this changed market has to come the realization that different requirements of purchase have to be called into play.

Today, when money is a problem, you have to learn to think like a real estate entrepreneur. You have to learn about financing, leverage, negotiating, brokers, and need-to-sell situations. Unfortunately, this education is not an overnight process. This book has been designed to set you off on a good start and stimulate your thinking in different areas that will help you in your house-buying pursuits. To supplement your education, make it a habit to talk to experienced and creative realtors, salespeople, real estate lawyers, and even home owners who've traveled the dollar-stretching route to ownership. Perhaps you could also arrange to meet with a creative real estate investor. Such an individual can be of invaluable help because the majority of them use these very same dollar-stretching techniques for investing in income properties. These strategies are the tools of the hard-nosed, leverage-oriented real estate investor. It only makes sense to see if you can consult with one of these individuals.

The time to get moving is now. Playing the waiting game will gain you nothing and may even work against your best interests.

Although mortgage interest rates from conventional lenders such as banks and savings and loan institutions may soften a bit and come down, several things ought to be considered. Mortgage interest rates move more slowly than other money interest rates, so even if greater interest rates are softening, mortgage interest rates will not come tumbling down at break-neck speed. This has been the general pattern in the past and it is logical to assume that it will be true in the future.

Moreover, the annual rate of appreciation in the price of homes is not tied to a national yardstick that can be consistently applied to all homes in all areas throughout the country. For example, when parts of California residential real estate were going berserk not too long ago, other areas in the country were moving along at a more rational 8, 10, or 12 percent appreciation rate. Some were even lagging behind that range of appreciation. What to many people would be a conservative and generally applicable rate of projected annual housing price appreciation, subject to local variations, is in the 10 percent range. In light of this kind of general projected appreciation, you have to weigh carefully the advantages of playing the waiting game for any amount of time. Then too, waiting means you'll be losing out on both the equity buildup and the tax deduction advantages of mortgage interest you would be getting if you became a home owner now.

In all likelihood, the higher price you pay for a house later might make your monthly payments on the mortgage higher even if rates were to soften somewhat. Suppose you're considering a $70,000 house on which you could get a 30-year mortgage for 80 percent of the price at 14 percent interest. Monthly payments would be $664 for interest and principal. If annual price appreciation is 10 percent and the interest rate drops to 13½ percent, your monthly mortgage payment will be $706. Not only will you be paying $42 a month more ($504 per year) but you will have lost out on one year's equity buildup and the tax advantages you would have had in deducting the interest part of your mortgage payments, and home prices might have gone up. Since interest is deductible, it may be cheaper, after taxes, to buy a house for a lower total price but at a higher interest rate than to wait and do the reverse.

You would have placed yourself one year behind on getting yourself onto what I've referred to in the book as the house-trade-up cycle. This concept has got to be one of the most important points we'll be making in this book, particularly if you're a first-time house buyer and what in essence we're saying here is: *It's imperative for you, if you're a first-time house buyer, to buy your first house as soon as possible in order that you can enter the trade-up cycle.* Therefore, it behooves you to beg, borrow, or steal to get the money and the financing in order to get ownership of your first house. It may not be your complete dream house, but it could well be the stepping stone that will eventually put you in the home of your dreams. After a year or so, when you've accumulated some equity, plus some additional cash through savings or moonlighting, you can sell or trade your house for a profit and scale up to a nicer house. The trick is to get started *now* and get yourself onto this house-buying merry-go-round or trading-up cycle!

This may appear to be an adverse time to be buying a house; however, consider the following. If mortgage rates subside, more potential home buyers will come into the market place and their buying demand will force the prices up faster. Also, it is in part high interest rates and high home prices that are adding to the inherent problems of the need-to-sell seller. While the sales market remains sluggish, the seller who has a genuine need-to-sell situation is vastly more interested in negotiating on price, terms, conditions, and financing.

In this regard, here are some additional sources for finding need-to-sell sellers. Lawyers involved in any inheritance where a house is part of the estate usually want to unload it fast. That could be a real home-buying find. Also, local bankers who have problem mortgage situations may be able to tell you about sellers interested in getting out from under. For another possibility, in every state there's a publication covering each community's real estate dealings (sales, mortgage loans, and so on). Under a hearing of *Lis Pendens* (a term that indicates a suit pending on the court docket), you'll find homes that are in trouble mortgage-wise, but that have not been foreclosed on. If you reach the property owner in time, you might be able to make an arrangement to buy his house that would be acceptable to him (because he would not lose his house through foreclosure), his banker, (because he too would avoid the referred to problems of foreclosure), and yourself because you might be able to make an advantageous purchase.

The biggest selling season for houses is spring and summer, and the slowest period is usually December, January, and February. A house listing that has gone through summer and fall without a sale could mean a more pliable seller in the deadly winter months when real estate activity virtually grinds to a halt. I know of several investors who buy houses and small rental properties in this slow period, walking into brokerage firms with as much available cash as they can to make advantageous purchases.

There's a strong possibility that today's current generation of first-time home buyers, being the product of the affluent 50's, 60's, and 70's, are less than realistic regarding what they can afford and what they can expect to find. Unfortunately, times do change and circumstances dictate that today's first-time house buyers will have to scale down their desires. In construction in the 80's, there will be more emphasis on the no-frills house with smaller rooms, no attic or fireplace and so on.

The important thing is to keep a proper set of priorities when entering the house-buying process. Learning to live with trade-offs of features and to look for financing arrangements you can live with is the order of the day. If you're looking for the perfect property in all your areas of consideration (size, style, condition, neighborhood, convenience, coupled with all your price, cash, and financing requirements), I suggest you're not going to find it! You're going to have to make some mental trade-offs for what is of *prime* importance to you (remembering all the time that your first purchase is not necessarily either your last nor your only home purchase, but merely an affordable home that will be able to offer you a degree of security, safety and comfort and, equally important, offering you the steppingstone means by which you can then move on to your next home which will be more to your liking). Many potential home buyers and weekend real estate investors who are looking for that perfect purchase or investment will still be looking for years to come!

GETTING STARTED

If you're looking to get into the trade-up cycle, then your entry level purchase might come from one of the shared living concepts—a condominium or cooperative or tandem house. Although these may represent compromise purchases, if you accept the trade-off concept you'll realize that these facilities could represent a practical means for you to get into the home-buying merry-go-round as equity builders. Remember, the next generation of first-time buyers, the ones coming into the house-buying market behind you, or the empty-nester looking for the minimal maintenance requirements, will in all likelihood be the buyers of *your* property. The market is growing rapidly for these kinds of properties as they continue to gain public acceptance. As a result, they will appreciate that much faster and your equity in the property will grow, giving you the potential dollars to go out and buy the new property that will come closer to your personal preferences.

With a condominium apartment, you own the unit outright in your own name and get a deed to it, just as with a house. In addition, you own an undivided interest in the condominium's common facilities. With a cooperative apartment, you own shares in the cooperative corporation in proportion to the size of your cooperative apartment unit. A tandem house, which is a relatively new concept, started in California, has two master bedrooms and a large kitchen and living room and is laid out so that two unrelated parties can own and occupy the house together. This kind of co-existence is not going to be everyone's cup of tea. Nonetheless it represents one more means for first-time home owners to get into the market.

When you're looking for a home that's in top-level condition, then its selling price is also going to be up to market. However, when you can latch onto a house that is in an acceptable neighborhood and that is structurally sound but in need of work, then the price on the property will reflect that fact. If you consider this kind of house, subject to an acceptable licensed physical inspection, you may be able to buy below market with favorable financing. Once you own the house, you can set the pace of what repairs you want to handle. In a sense, such a property gives you the opportunity to gradually bring the house up to its real market value. That's another way of expressing the established real estate concept: "Always buy the worst-looking property in the nicest neighborhood you can afford." You can't change a neighborhood, but you can in all likelihood improve a neglected home and, in so doing, increase your equity in the property tremendously. The house that looks awful turns most prospective buyers off, but to the trained real estate entrepreneur it spells opportunity.

Many first-time home owners look into buying an older home as a means of getting into the home ownership market. It's usually 10 to 25 percent cheaper to buy an older home than a new one because newer homes reflect the higher costs of material, labor, and financing. In the older home category, you might also want to look into buying a two- or three-family house as a means of entree. If you can handle what will be your dual role of landlord and neighbor as well as your mortgage payments as owner, then this might be an excellent way for you to get into home ownership.

In the new-home market, smaller, no-frills homes on smaller lots are being built which might put them in the affordable price and financing category for you. Also, often overextended builders of new homes wind up in the need-to-sell category and are more amenable to price and financing arrangements that can mean the affordable house you've been looking for.

Some other alternatives are mobile homes on permanent foundations; homes where outside investors work out an equity arrangement with the owners; homes where the building is bought but the land underneath is merely leased; and Planned Unit Development, an arrangement whereby you own a home on a tiny lot and also share in a larger, separate piece of land through a home owner's association. Changing economic times will bring about *more* modifications in houses and styles of living to accommodate the changing economic needs of home owners.

Today, there are many techniques and strategies available to help you buy an affordable house. You simply have to be willing to:

1. Do your homework. Take the time to learn and absorb the different strategies introduced in this book.

2. Apply these principles. They can work for you as they have for thousands of others. As a savvy buyer, unafraid to negotiate for the lowest price with advantageous financing in need-to-sell situations, you can pick up bargains in new and resale homes and condominiums that weren't available in prior years.

The concepts of dollar stretching, low-cash buying, and searching out need-to-sell situations are, and will continue to be, as valid tomorrow as they are today. If your desire to buy a house is strong and if you're willing to take the time to learn the needed strategies and apply them, you *will* stand an excellent chance of finding and buying that affordable house!

Good luck in your home buying pursuits!

INDEX

164

MENTOR Titles of Interest

Exciting Fiction from SIGNET

(0451)

- [ ] **THE DEVIL TO PAY by Earl Thompson.** (119096—$3.95)*
- [ ] **RED SUNSET by John Stockwell.** (119126—$3.50)*
- [ ] **HEADING WEST by Doris Betts.** (119134—$3.50)*
- [ ] **DEATH BY GASLIGHT by Michael Kurland.** (119150—$3.50)*
- [ ] **HEART CHANGE by Lynn Freed.** (119169—$3.50)*
- [ ] **FEVER by Robin Cook.** (119932—$3.95)*
- [ ] **NIGHT CALL FROM A DISTANT TIME ZONE by Herbert Lieberman.** (119940—$3.50)*
- [ ] **SHAWNEE DAWN (The Indian Heritage Series #2) by Paul Joseph Lederer.** (120000—$2.95)*
- [ ] **WINTER LORD by Jean Brooks-Janowiak.** (120027—$2.95)*
- [ ] **FALLBACK by Peter Niesewand.** (120531—$3.95)*
- [ ] **NIGHT SANCTUARY by Monique Van Vooren.** (120558—$3.95)*
- [ ] **WATCHDOG by Faith Sullivan.** (120566—$2.95)*
- [ ] **THE MEDUSA SYNDROME by Ron Cutler.** (120574—$2.95)*
- [ ] **WINTER OF THE WHITE SEAL by Marie Herbert.** (120612—$3.50)†
- [ ] **THE NIGHT CHASERS by Jamey Cohen.** (120604—$3.50)*

*Prices slightly higher in Canada
†Not available in Canada

Buy them at your local bookstore or use this convenient coupon for ordering.

THE NEW AMERICAN LIBRARY, INC.,
P.O. Box 999, Bergenfield, New Jersey 07621

Please send me the books I have checked above. I am enclosing $_____
(please add $1.00 to this order to cover postage and handling). Send check
or money order—no cash or C.O.D.'s. Prices and numbers are subject to change
without notice.

Name_____

Address_____

City _____ State _____ Zip Code _____
Allow 4-6 weeks for delivery.
This offer is subject to withdrawal without notice.